MW01296940

# A CHRISTIAN'S FIVE-YEAR JOURNAL

## DENNIS CRAVENS

WESTBOW°
PRESS
A DIVISION OF THOMAS NELSON
& ZONDERVAN

Copyright © 2014 Dennis Cravens.

All rights reserved. No part of this book may be used or reproduced by any means, graphic, electronic, or mechanical, including photocopying, recording, taping or by any information storage retrieval system without the written permission of the publisher except in the case of brief quotations embodied in critical articles and reviews.

All Scripture quotations, unless otherwise indicated, are taken from the American King James Version (AKJV) that was placed into public domain on November 8, 1999 by Michael Peter Engelbrite. The AKJV is a simple word-for-word update from the King James Version using modernized wording but without alterations of grammar and doctrine.

WestBow Press books may be ordered through booksellers or by contacting:

WestBow Press
A Division of Thomas Nelson & Zondervan
1663 Liberty Drive
Bloomington, IN 47403
www.westbowpress.com
1 (866) 928-1240

Because of the dynamic nature of the Internet, any web addresses or links contained in this book may have changed since publication and may no longer be valid. The views expressed in this work are solely those of the author and do not necessarily reflect the views of the publisher, and the publisher hereby disclaims any responsibility for them.

Any people depicted in stock imagery provided by Thinkstock are models, and such images are being used for illustrative purposes only.
Certain stock imagery © Thinkstock.

ISBN: 978-1-4908-2705-6 (sc)
ISBN: 978-1-4908-2707-0 (hc)
ISBN: 978-1-4908-2706-3 (e)

Library of Congress Control Number: 2014903042

Printed in the United States of America.

WestBow Press rev. date: 3/6/2014

Your name

# A Christian's Five-Year Journal

## Dennis Cravens

Finally, brothers: whatever things are true, whatever things are honest, whatever things are just, whatever things are pure, whatever things are lovely, whatever things are of good report; if there be any virtue, and if there be any praise, think on these things.

**Philippians 4:8**

# INTRODUCTION

We all have ups and downs. "The voyage of the best ship is a zigzag line of a hundred tacks. See the line from a sufficient distance, and it straightens itself to the average tendency." (Emerson in *Self Reliance*).

Are you on track? Are you moving to your destination? Do you have a clear idea what your destination is? This book helps you see your life from the distance of time. It doesn't take a lot of time or lengthy journal entries. Just read the supplied verse each day and then answer a question for that day's date. After the first year, you will see what you were thinking or doing on the same day in previous years. You will find it encouraging knowing that you have grown and gained insight. If you haven't, then it shows where you need to work. But mostly it should help you focus on your Christian life and give you a little structure for thinking on a verse each day in a way that you can personally apply to your life.

## VERSES

All Scripture quotations, unless otherwise indicated, are taken from the American King James Version (AKJV) that was placed into public domain on November 8, 1999 by Michael Peter Engelbrite. The AKJV is a simple word-for-word update from the King James Version using modernized wording but without alterations of grammar and doctrine often seen in many modern revisions. You will notice that some scriptures quoted may end without periods or with punctuations other than a period. The punctuation at the end of the quote is retained from the AKJV. Ellipses (…) indicate part of the verse was omitted due to space.

# How to use this Book

The hardest part of this, or any journal, is developing the habit. The best way to establish a habit is to append it to an existing habit. Try reading and writing after you brush your teeth or take your medicine or watch the news. That is, use something you always do as a trigger to develop this new habit. For example put the journal under your TV remote and read the verse and write a sentence as you put the remote up for the night or put it by the cat food and use the journal after you feed the cat. The method I recommend is to put it by your morning items, and read the verse and question before you comb your hair, take a shower, or whatever. Think about the verse and question as you do your morning activity. Then when you finish jot down a quick response. The idea is to make journaling a part of something you already do habitually. In about a month it will become part of you.

The instructions are simple: First, read the verse. Next think for a minute and finally answer the question(s). That's all. You don't need to write a novel. You may want to keep it simple with just a yes or no when you first start. How much and how you answer is part of the experience. As Ecclesiastes 9:4 says, "A living dog is better than a dead lion." The idea is to do something and do it continually. If all you have time for is a yes or no, a name or a single word, then so be it. As you grow, you will find yourself giving more open and revealing answers. That is part of the process.

You don't need to think up flowery words. Just answer the question and turn your journal entry into a daily habit. If you make it long and hard then you are apt to stop. The goal here is growth and long range continuity.

After the first year, return to the same date and answer the question again. See how you have grown and changed over the year(s). You might find your views of the verse are different. You will likely see new applications.

Some questions are easy but most are designed to make you think. The answers are for you- to see how you have grown - to make you think - to move you to good works - to help you grow — so just be honest and open.

# Did you miss a day?

Face it, there will be times when you forget or misplace your pencil or you are too much in a hurry to take the time. This journal is for you. Do it your own way. There is nothing wrong with going back and filling in missing days. I advise you to try making a simple entry each day because it makes the habit stronger. But there is nothing wrong in doing it once a week or some other uniquely personal way.

# Special Occasions

There are a few pages in the back of the journal for special events e. g., birthdays, anniverseries, births, graduation, weddings, funerals, financial loss, new home, additional notes, and for resolutions for the next year.

# Notes

One thing you might want to do when you first start the journal is to add personal reminders on special days. For example, enter things like birthday and anniversary reminders to the notes at the bottom of the pages.

# About the Author

Dr. Dennis Cravens received his BS from Abilene Christian College in 1973 and later a PhD from Florida State University in 1977. Although his degree is in Molecular Biophysics, he has been a part time preacher and a deacon, for many years and "fills in" for the local preacher and song leader. He has taught at Christian colleges for 38 years and has developed several Bible friendly science courses for Christian Universities affiliated with the Church of Christ.

He has found that grandiose plans often fail in the long term, but simple things like focusing on a single verse each day is practical and sustainable year after year. This journal is designed with the concept that doing something simple is better than all the best intentions (see the second chapter of James). He is now working on a book based on the Wisdom Books of the Bible.

# 1 JANUARY

**Ecclesiastes 3:2-3** A time to be born, and a time to die; a time to plant, and a time to pluck up that which is planted; A time to kill, and a time to heal; a time to break down, and a time to build up;

Is there something you need to tear down and just start over?

**Year One**        20____

**Year Two**        20____

**Year Three**      20____

**Year Four**       20____

**Year Five**       20____

**Notes**

JANUARY 2

**Matthew 5:4** Blessed are they that mourn, for they shall be comforted

Have you sought to comfort anyone this week? Who?

Year One        20____

Year Two        20____

Year Three      20____

Year Four       20____

Year Five       20____

Notes

5

# 3 JANUARY

**Romans 12:17** Recompense to no man evil for evil. Provide things honest in the sight of all men.

How have you returned good for an evil done to you?

Year One          20____

_____

Year Two          20____

_____

Year Three        20____

_____

Year Four         20____

_____

Year Five         20____

_____

Notes

_____

**Proverbs 31:21** She is not afraid of the snow for her household: for all her household are clothed with scarlet.

Have you taken measures to take care of your family during times of trouble?

Year One        20____

_____

_____

Year Two        20____

_____

_____

Year Three      20____

_____

_____

Year Four       20____

_____

_____

Year Five       20____

_____

_____

Notes

_____

_____

_____

# 5 JANUARY

**Psalms 116:1-2** I love the LORD, because he has heard my voice and my supplications. Because he has inclined his ear to me, therefore will I call on him as long as I live.

Do you always remember to call on the Lord? When was the last time?

**Year One**        20____

---

**Year Two**        20____

---

**Year Three**      20____

---

**Year Four**       20____

---

**Year Five**       20____

---

**Notes**

---

**Isaiah 41:10** Fear you not; for I am with you: be not dismayed; for I am your God: I will strengthen you; yes, I will help you; yes, I will uphold you with the right hand of my righteousness.

With what do you want God to strengthen and help you? Have you asked?

Year One        20____

Year Two        20____

Year Three      20____

Year Four       20____

Year Five       20____

Notes

# 7 JANUARY

**Psalms 119:50** This is my comfort in my affliction: for your word has strengthened me.

What is God's promise to you?

**Year One**     20____

_____

_____

**Year Two**     20____

_____

_____

**Year Three**    20____

_____

_____

**Year Four**    20____

_____

_____

**Year Five**    20____

_____

_____

**Notes**

_____

_____

_____

**2 Corinthians 12:9** And he said to me, My grace is sufficient for you: for my strength is made perfect in weakness. Most gladly therefore will I rather glory in my infirmities, that the power of Christ may rest on me.

What is your weakness and how can you let God use it?

Year One        20____

Year Two        20____

Year Three      20____

Year Four       20____

Year Five       20____

Notes

# 9 JANUARY

**Matthew 7:7** Ask, and it shall be given you; seek, and you shall find; knock, and it shall be opened to you

What do you seek right now?

**Year One**      20___

_____

_____

**Year Two**      20___

_____

_____

**Year Three**      20___

_____

_____

**Year Four**      20___

_____

_____

**Year Five**      20___

_____

_____

**Notes**

_____

_____

_____

**Proverbs 11:14** Where no counsel is, the people fall: but in the multitude of counselors there is safety.

To whom do you go for advice?

Year One        20\_\_\_\_

Year Two        20\_\_\_\_

Year Three      20\_\_\_\_

Year Four       20\_\_\_\_

Year Five       20\_\_\_\_

Notes

# 11 JANUARY

**Isaiah 43:18** Don't remember the former things, neither consider the things of old.

Do you seek to forgive and forget?

Year One        20____

_____

_____

Year Two        20____

_____

_____

Year Three      20____

_____

_____

Year Four       20____

_____

_____

Year Five       20____

_____

_____

_____

Notes

_____

_____

_____

**Romans 8:28** And we know that all things work together for good to them that love God, to them who are the called according to his purpose.

Give an example how things have worked to your good.

Year One        20____

_____

_____

Year Two        20____

_____

_____

Year Three      20____

_____

_____

Year Four       20____

_____

_____

Year Five       20____

_____

_____

Notes

_____

_____

# 13 JANUARY

**Proverbs 19:11** The Wise defers his anger; and it is his glory to pass over a transgression.

Have you overlooked someone's offense this week?

Year One      20____

_____

_____

Year Two      20____

_____

_____

Year Three    20____

_____

_____

Year Four     20____

_____

_____

Year Five     20____

_____

_____

Notes

_____

_____

_____

**Galatians 5:22-25** But the fruit of the Spirit is love, joy, peace, long-suffering, gentleness, goodness, faith, meekness, temperance: against such there is no law.

When were you last gentle to someone else?

Year One          20\_\_\_\_

Year Two          20\_\_\_\_

Year Three        20\_\_\_\_

Year Four         20\_\_\_\_

Year Five         20\_\_\_\_

Notes

# 15 JANUARY

**Proverbs 16:3** Commit your work to the LORD and your thoughts will be established.

What work do you do just for the Lord?

Year One        20____

Year Two        20____

Year Three      20____

Year Four       20____

Year Five       20____

Notes

**1 Peter 5:6-7** Humble yourselves therefore under the mighty hand of God, that he may exalt you in due time: Casting all your care on him; for he cares for you.

What anxiety have you turned over to God?

**Year One**       20____

_____

_____

**Year Two**       20____

_____

_____

**Year Three**     20____

_____

_____

**Year Four**      20____

_____

_____

**Year Five**      20____

_____

_____

**Notes**

_____

_____

_____

# 17 JANUARY

**Psalms 19:14** Let the words of my mouth, and the meditation of my heart, be acceptable in your sight, O LORD, my strength, and my redeemer.

What have you meditated on today?

Year One        20___

Year Two        20___

Year Three      20___

Year Four       20___

Year Five       20___

Notes

**Acts 4:11** This is the stone which was set at nothing of you builders, which is become the head of the corner.

Who have you found hidden or unexpected value in?

Year One       20____

Year Two       20____

Year Three     20____

Year Four      20____

Year Five      20____

Notes

**Psalm 119:105** Your word is a lamp to my feet, and a light for my path.

How has the word lightened your feet so far this year?

**Year One**      20_____

---

**Year Two**      20_____

---

**Year Three**    20_____

---

**Year Four**     20_____

---

**Year Five**     20_____

---

**Notes**

---

**Matthew 5:9** Blessed are the peacemakers: for they shall be called the children of God.

How have you tried to make peace this month?

Year One        20____

Year Two        20____

Year Three      20____

Year Four       20____

Year Five       20____

Notes

# 21 JANUARY

**1 John 3:17** But whoever has this world's goods, and sees his brother have need, and closes his heart to him, how does the love of God live in him?

What do you have that you can share or give to another?

**Year One**    20____

_____

_____

**Year Two**    20____

_____

_____

**Year Three**    20____

_____

_____

**Year Four**    20____

_____

_____

**Year Five**    20____

_____

_____

**Notes**

_____

_____

_____

**Romans 8:26** Likewise the Spirit also helps our weaknesses: for we know not what we should pray for as we should: but the Spirit itself intercedes for us with groanings which cannot be uttered.

Do you often have something that you cannot express in words?

Year One          20____

Year Two          20____

Year Three        20____

Year Four         20____

Year Five         20____

Notes

# 23 JANUARY

**Psalms 46:1** God is our refuge and strength, a very present help in trouble.

What do you need or what to take refuge from?

Year One          20____
.................................................................................

Year Two          20____
.................................................................................

Year Three        20____
.................................................................................

Year Four         20____
.................................................................................

Year Five         20____
.................................................................................

Notes
.................................................................................

**Genesis 1:26** And God said, Let us make man in our image, after our likeness …

What do you look for when you want to see the image of God in others?

Year One        20____

Year Two        20____

Year Three      20____

Year Four       20____

Year Five       20____

Notes

# 25 JANUARY

**Psalms 143:10** Teach me to do your will; for you are my God: your spirit is good; lead me into the land of uprightness.

Where is God leading you?

**Year One**  20____

_____

_____

**Year Two**  20____

_____

_____

**Year Three**  20____

_____

_____

**Year Four**  20____

_____

_____

**Year Five**  20____

_____

_____

**Notes**

_____

_____

**2 John 1:6** And this is love, that we walk after his commandments.

Do you love the Lord enough to obey his commandments? Name one of his commandments.

Year One        20____

Year Two        20____

Year Three      20____

Year Four       20____

Year Five       20____

Notes

**Proverbs 29:1** He, that stiffens his neck against criticism, shall suddenly be destroyed, and that without remedy.

How have you been criticized lately? Did you take it yielding or stiff necked?

**Year One**          20____

_____

_____

**Year Two**          20____

_____

_____

**Year Three**        20____

_____

_____

**Year Four**         20____

_____

_____

**Year Five**         20____

_____

_____

**Notes**

_____

_____

_____

**1 John 1:8** If we say that we have no sin, we deceive ourselves, and the truth is not in us.

Do you freely admit your mistakes? What was the last fault you admitted?

**Year One**        20____

_____

_____

**Year Two**        20____

_____

_____

**Year Three**      20____

_____

_____

**Year Four**       20____

_____

_____

**Year Five**       20____

_____

_____

**Notes**

_____

_____

_____

**James 3:18** And the fruit of righteousness is sown in peace by those who make peace.

Have you tried to make peace with others? How?

Year One          20____

Year Two          20____

Year Three        20____

Year Four         20____

Year Five         20____

Notes

**Philippians 1:3-4** I thank my God on every remembrance of you, Always in every prayer of mine for you all making request with joy,

Who was the last person you prayed for?

Year One          20____

_____

_____

Year Two          20____

_____

_____

Year Three        20____

_____

_____

Year Four         20____

_____

_____

Year Five         20____

_____

_____

Notes

_____

_____

_____

# 31 JANUARY

**Jeremiah 33:12** Thus said the LORD of hosts; Again in this place, which is desolate without man and without beast, and in all the cities thereof, shall be a habitation of shepherds causing their flocks to lie down.

When was the last time you arranged for others to rest?

Year One          20____

_____

_____

Year Two          20____

_____

_____

Year Three       20____

_____

_____

Year Four        20____

_____

_____

Year Five        20____

_____

_____

Notes

_____

_____

**Psalm 55:6** And I said, Oh that I had wings like a dove! for then would I fly away, and be at rest.

From what would you like to escape right now?

**Year One**     20____

_____

_____

**Year Two**     20____

_____

_____

**Year Three**     20____

_____

_____

**Year Four**     20____

_____

_____

**Year Five**     20____

_____

_____

**Notes**

_____

_____

_____

# 2   FEBRUARY

**Isaiah 26:3** You will keep him in perfect peace, whose mind is stayed on you: because he trusts in you.

What did you spend most of your time thinking about yesterday?

**Year One**　　　20____

_____

_____

**Year Two**　　　20____

_____

_____

**Year Three**　　20____

_____

_____

**Year Four**　　　20____

_____

_____

**Year Five**　　　20____

_____

_____

**Notes**

_____

_____

_____

**Luke 16:10** He that is faithful in that which is small is faithful also in much: and he that is unjust in the small is unjust also in much.

What little matters have you worked on this week (or plan to work on this week)?

**Year One**     20____

_____

_____

**Year Two**     20____

_____

_____

**Year Three**     20____

_____

_____

**Year Four**     20____

_____

_____

**Year Five**     20____

_____

_____

**Notes**

_____

_____

_____

**2 Corinthians 4:18** While we look not at the things which are seen, but at the things which are not seen: for the things which are seen are temporal; but the things which are not seen are eternal.

What is your eye "fixed upon"?

**Year One**        20____

................................................................................................................

................................................................................................................

**Year Two**        20____

................................................................................................................

................................................................................................................

**Year Three**      20____

................................................................................................................

................................................................................................................

**Year Four**       20____

................................................................................................................

................................................................................................................

**Year Five**       20____

................................................................................................................

................................................................................................................

**Notes**

................................................................................................................

................................................................................................................

................................................................................................................

**Luke 11:28** But he said, Yes rather, blessed are they that hear the word of God, and keep it.

When do you seek times to listen to the word of God?

Year One          20____

_____

_____

Year Two          20____

_____

_____

Year Three       20____

_____

_____

Year Four        20____

_____

_____

Year Five        20____

_____

_____

Notes

_____

_____

_____

**Colossians 3:12** Put on therefore, as the chosen of God, holy and beloved, compassion, kindness, humbleness of mind, meekness, long-suffering;

When did you last show compassion?

**Year One**        20____

_____

_____

**Year Two**        20____

_____

_____

**Year Three**        20____

_____

_____

**Year Four**        20____

_____

_____

**Year Five**        20____

_____

_____

**Notes**

_____

_____

**Colossians 3:13** Forbearing one another, and forgiving one another, if any man have a quarrel against any: even as Christ forgave you, so also do you...

Do you always forgive or just sometimes and some people? Is there someone you need to forgive right now?

**Year One**    20____

_____

_____

**Year Two**    20____

_____

_____

**Year Three**    20____

_____

_____

**Year Four**    20____

_____

_____

**Year Five**    20____

_____

_____

**Notes**

_____

_____

# 8  FEBRUARY

**1 John 3:18** My little children, let us not love in word, neither in tongue; but in deed and in truth.

Do you actually do good deeds or just talk about doing them some day? What good deed did you do this week?

**Year One**        20____

_____

_____

_____

**Year Two**        20____

_____

_____

_____

**Year Three**      20____

_____

_____

_____

**Year Four**       20____

_____

_____

_____

**Year Five**       20____

_____

_____

_____

**Notes**

_____

_____

_____

**James 5:16** Confess your faults one to another, and pray one for another, that you may be healed.

When was the last time you confessed a fault?

Year One        20____

_____

_____

Year Two        20____

_____

_____

Year Three      20____

_____

_____

Year Four       20____

_____

_____

Year Five       20____

_____

_____

Notes

_____

_____

_____

# 10 FEBRUARY

**Proverbs 25:23** The north wind drives away rain: so does an angry countenance a backbiting tongue.

Have you engaged in telling negative things about another?

Year One         20____

_____

_____

Year Two         20____

_____

_____

Year Three       20____

_____

_____

Year Four        20____

_____

_____

Year Five        20____

_____

_____

Notes

_____

_____

**Psalms 126:3** The LORD has done great things for us; so we are glad.

What great thing has the Lord done for you?

**Year One**       20\_\_\_\_

_____

_____

**Year Two**       20\_\_\_\_

_____

_____

**Year Three**     20\_\_\_\_

_____

_____

**Year Four**      20\_\_\_\_

_____

_____

**Year Five**      20\_\_\_\_

_____

_____

**Notes**

_____

_____

_____

# 12 FEBRUARY

**Psalms 56:8** You know my wanderings: put you my tears into your bottle: are they not in your book?

What did you cry about last time?

Year One        20____

_____

_____

Year Two        20____

_____

_____

Year Three      20____

_____

_____

Year Four       20____

_____

_____

Year Five       20____

_____

_____

Notes

_____

_____

_____

**Romans 8:6** For to be carnally minded is death; but to be spiritually minded is life and peace.

What is your mind set on? How specifically?

**Year One**       20____

_____

_____

**Year Two**       20____

_____

_____

**Year Three**     20____

_____

_____

**Year Four**      20____

_____

_____

**Year Five**      20____

_____

_____

**Notes**

_____

_____

_____

**Genesis 29:20** And Jacob served seven years for Rachel; and they seemed to him but a few days, for the love he had to her.

How fast does time pass when you are with the one you love?

Year One          20____

_____

_____

Year Two          20____

_____

_____

Year Three        20____

_____

_____

Year Four         20____

_____

_____

Year Five         20____

_____

_____

Notes

_____

_____

**1 Corinthians 13:4** Love is patient and kind.

How long do you love others without it being returned?

Year One         20\_\_\_\_

Year Two         20\_\_\_\_

Year Three       20\_\_\_\_

Year Four        20\_\_\_\_

Year Five        20\_\_\_\_

Notes

# 16 FEBRUARY

**Genesis 2:9** And out of the ground made the LORD God to grow every tree that is pleasant to the sight, and good for food;

Have you ever planted or made something for another? What/when?

**Year One**    20____

_____

_____

**Year Two**    20____

_____

_____

**Year Three**    20____

_____

_____

**Year Four**    20____

_____

_____

**Year Five**    20____

_____

_____

**Notes**

_____

_____

**Psalm 23:4** Yes, though I walk through the valley of the shadow of death, I will fear no evil:

Do you fear death? Why/why not?

**Year One**      20____

**Year Two**      20____

**Year Three**      20____

**Year Four**      20____

**Year Five**      20____

**Notes**

# 18   F<small>EBRUARY</small>

**1 Corinthians 1:4** I thank my God always on your behalf, for the grace of God which is given you by Jesus Christ;

Who are you thankful that you have known? Have you told them?

**Year One**      20____

_____

_____

**Year Two**      20____

_____

_____

**Year Three**      20____

_____

_____

**Year Four**      20____

_____

_____

**Year Five**      20____

_____

_____

**Notes**

_____

_____

**Psalm 66:17** I cried to him with my mouth, and he was extolled with my tongue.

How did you praise the LORD in your last prayer?

Year One          20____

Year Two          20____

Year Three       20____

Year Four         20____

Year Five          20____

Notes

# 20 FEBRUARY

**Matthew 6:26** Behold the fowls of the air: for they sow not, neither do they reap, nor gather into barns; yet your heavenly Father feeds them. Are you not much better than they?

What are you thankful for today that the Lord has provided?

Year One          20____

Year Two          20____

Year Three        20____

Year Four         20____

Year Five         20____

Notes

**Philippians 4:4** Rejoice in the Lord always: and again I say, Rejoice.

Write a sentence of rejoicing.

Year One          20____

Year Two          20____

Year Three       20____

Year Four         20____

Year Five          20____

Notes

**Isaiah 48:3** I have declared the former things from the beginning; and they went forth out of my mouth, and I showed them; I did them suddenly, and they came to pass...

What should you have done or said that you have not? When will you do it?

Year One          20____

_____

_____

Year Two          20____

_____

_____

Year Three        20____

_____

_____

Year Four         20____

_____

_____

Year Five         20____

_____

_____

Notes

_____

_____

**Psalms 119:48** My hands also will I lift up to your commandments, which I have loved; and I will meditate in your statutes.

How often do you meditate on God's word?

Year One        20____

Year Two        20____

Year Three      20____

Year Four       20____

Year Five       20____

Notes

# 24 FEBRUARY

**Philippians 4:19** But my God shall supply all your need according to his riches in glory by Christ Jesus.

Name a need you have that God has recently supplied?

**Year One**        20____

**Year Two**        20____

**Year Three**      20____

**Year Four**       20____

**Year Five**       20____

**Notes**

**Psalms 73:26** My flesh and my heart fails: but God is the strength of my heart, and my portion forever.

How is your heart and mind stronger and more trustworthy than your physical strength?

Year One        20____

Year Two        20____

Year Three      20____

Year Four       20____

Year Five       20____

Notes

# 26 February

**Proverbs 13:13** Whoever despises the word shall be destroyed: but he that fears the commandment shall be rewarded.

Do you delight in following the word because you love God and want to please him or look for loopholes?

**Year One**        20____

_____

_____

**Year Two**        20____

_____

_____

**Year Three**        20____

_____

_____

**Year Four**        20____

_____

_____

**Year Five**        20____

_____

_____

**Notes**

_____

_____

**Revelation 21:3** And I heard a great voice out of heaven saying, Behold, the tabernacle of God is with men, and he will dwell with them

Is God dwelling in you? How do you know?

Year One        20____

Year Two        20____

Year Three        20____

Year Four        20____

Year Five        20____

Notes

# 28 FEBRUARY

**2 John 1:12** Having many things to write to you, I would not write with paper and ink: but I trust to come to you, and speak face to face, that our joy may be full.

Do you make it a point to talk to people sometimes to express things or always just use the computer?

**Year One**        20___

**Year Two**        20___

**Year Three**      20___

**Year Four**       20___

**Year Five**       20___

**Notes**

**1 Peter 4:16** Yet if any man suffer as a Christian, let him not be ashamed; but let him glorify God on this behalf.

Have you (or someone you know) suffered as a Christian? How?

Year One        20____

_____

_____

Year Two        20____

_____

_____

Year Three      20____

_____

_____

Year Four       20____

_____

_____

Year Five       20____

_____

_____

Notes

_____

_____

# 1 MARCH

**James 4:8** Draw close to God, and he will draw close to you.

When do you feel closest to God?

Year One        20____

Year Two        20____

Year Three      20____

Year Four       20____

Year Five       20____

Notes

**Galatians 5:14** For all the law is fulfilled in one word, even in this; you shall love your neighbor as yourself.

How have you shown love to your neighbor this week?

Year One        20____

_____

_____

Year Two        20____

_____

_____

Year Three      20____

_____

_____

Year Four       20____

_____

_____

Year Five       20____

_____

_____

Notes

_____

_____

_____

# 3 MARCH

**Ephesians 5:33** Nevertheless let every one of you in particular so love his wife even as himself; and let the wife show reverence her husband.

How have you shown love to your spouse or friend today?

**Year One**      20____

_____

_____

**Year Two**      20____

_____

_____

**Year Three**    20____

_____

_____

**Year Four**     20____

_____

_____

**Year Five**     20____

_____

_____

**Notes**

_____

_____

**1 John 3:16** Hereby we know the love of God, because he laid down his life for us: and we ought to lay down our lives for the brothers.

For what or whom are you willing to die?

Year One        20____

Year Two        20____

Year Three      20____

Year Four       20____

Year Five       20____

Notes

# 5 MARCH

**Genesis 2:2-3** And on the seventh day God ended his work which he had made; and he rested on the seventh day from all his work…

When was the last time you rested from your work?

Year One        20____

Year Two        20____

Year Three        20____

Year Four        20____

Year Five        20____

Notes

**Genesis 22:14** So Abraham called the name of that place, "The LORD will provide";

What has the Lord unexpectedly provided you that you could not have expected by logic alone?

Year One        20____

Year Two        20____

Year Three      20____

Year Four       20____

Year Five       20____

Notes

# 7 MARCH

**Psalms 86:5** For you, O Lord, are good and ready to forgive, and plenteous in mercy to all them that call on you.

Do you trust God when he says he will forgive? Do you still live with guilt and doubts? About what?

Year One        20____

Year Two        20____

Year Three      20____

Year Four       20____

Year Five       20____

Notes

**Proverbs 30:4** Who has ascended to heaven and
descended?… What is his name, and what is his son's name?

Jesus!

Of whom does this speak? Surely you know, but it is good to proclaim it.
When did you last tell another?

Year One      20 16

When did I last tell another? Last night @
BSF. But when did I tell a neighbour or
a stranger? Very convicting...

Year Two      20___

Year Three    20___

Year Four     20___

Year Five     20___

Notes

# 9 MARCH

**Jonah 2:9** I will pay that that I have vowed. Salvation is of the LORD. But I will sacrifice to you with the voice of thanksgiving

What promise have you made to God that you need yet to keep?

Year One          20____

Year Two          20____

Year Three        20____

Year Four         20____

Year Five         20____

Notes

**Luke 10:** 42 …and Mary has chosen that good part, which shall not be taken away from her…

Do you still honor God even in a crowd or stay troubled with things of life?

Year One        20____

Year Two        20____

Year Three      20____

Year Four       20____

Year Five       20____

Notes

# 11 MARCH

**1 Corinthians 3:11** For other foundation can no man lay than has been laid, which is Jesus Christ.

What are you building on your foundation or does it remain empty? What would you want on your foundation?

**Year One**       20____

_____

_____

**Year Two**       20____

_____

_____

**Year Three**       20____

_____

_____

**Year Four**       20____

_____

_____

**Year Five**       20____

_____

_____

**Notes**

_____

_____

_____

**Genesis 46:3-4** And he said, I am God, the God of your father. Do not be afraid to go down to Egypt… I will go with you…

How do you take God with you in all your travels?

**Year One**        20____

_____

_____

**Year Two**        20____

_____

_____

**Year Three**      20____

_____

_____

**Year Four**       20____

_____

_____

**Year Five**       20____

_____

_____

**Notes**

_____

_____

_____

# 13 MARCH

**John 16:21** A woman when she is in travail has sorrow, because her hour is come: but as soon as she is delivered of the child, she remembers no more the anguish, for joy that a man is born into the world.

Have you found joy at a birth? Whose, when?

Year One          20____

Year Two          20____

Year Three        20____

Year Four         20____

Year Five         20____

Notes

**1 Peter 1:8-9** Whom having not seen, you love; in whom, though now you see him not, yet believing, you rejoice with joy unspeakable and full of glory:

How hard is it for you to believe in what you cannot see?

Year One        20____

_____

_____

Year Two        20____

_____

_____

Year Three      20____

_____

_____

Year Four       20____

_____

_____

Year Five       20____

_____

_____

Notes

_____

_____

# 15 MARCH

**2 Thessalonians 3:6** Now we command you, brethren, in the name of our Lord Jesus Christ, that you withdraw yourselves from every brother that walks disorderly

Is there someone that is being a bad influence for you? How are you handing it?

Year One        20____

_____

_____

Year Two        20____

_____

_____

Year Three      20____

_____

_____

Year Four       20____

_____

_____

Year Five       20____

_____

_____

Notes

_____

_____

_____

**Hebrews 13:17** Obey them that have the rule over you…

Do you find it hard to obey some rules? Which ones?

Year One        20____

Year Two        20____

Year Three      20____

Year Four       20____

Year Five       20____

Notes

# 17 MARCH

**John 14:15** If you love me, keep my commandments

Do you love the Lord with all your heart? How do you show it?

**Year One** 20___

_____

_____

**Year Two** 20___

_____

_____

**Year Three** 20___

_____

_____

**Year Four** 20___

_____

_____

**Year Five** 20___

_____

_____

**Notes**

_____

_____

**Galatians 5:13** For, brothers, you have been called to liberty; only use not liberty for an occasion to the flesh, but by love serve one another.

Do you use your humanity as an excuse for some of your actions? Which actions?

Year One        20____

Year Two        20____

Year Three      20____

Year Four       20____

Year Five       20____

Notes

# 19 MARCH

**Zechariah 8:16** These are the things that you shall do; Speak you every man the truth to his neighbor; execute the judgment of truth and peace in your gates:

Do you always speak the truth? When did you last find it hard to tell the truth?

**Year One**        20____

_____

_____

**Year Two**        20____

_____

_____

**Year Three**      20____

_____

_____

**Year Four**       20____

_____

_____

**Year Five**       20____

_____

_____

**Notes**

_____

_____

_____

**1 Corinthians 6:12** All things are lawful to me, but all things are not expedient: all things are lawful for me, but I will not be brought under the power of any.

What seeks to force power over you?

**Year One**       20____

_____

_____

**Year Two**       20____

_____

_____

**Year Three**     20____

_____

_____

**Year Four**      20____

_____

_____

**Year Five**      20____

_____

_____

**Notes**

_____

_____

_____

# 21 MARCH

**Isaiah 1:18** Come now, let us reason together, says the LORD: though your sins are like scarlet, they shall be as white as snow; though they are red like crimson, they shall become like wool.

How do you feel knowing your sins are forgiven?

Year One        20____
_____

Year Two        20____
_____

Year Three      20____
_____

Year Four       20____
_____

Year Five       20____
_____

Notes
_____

**James 1:6** But let him ask in faith, nothing doubting. For he that doubts is like a wave of the sea driven with the wind and tossed.

What do you pray for that you have absolutely no doubt about?

Year One          20____

_____

_____

Year Two          20____

_____

_____

Year Three        20____

_____

_____

Year Four         20____

_____

_____

Year Five         20____

_____

_____

Notes

_____

_____

# 23 MARCH

**Romans 12:10** Love one another with brotherly love; in honor preferring one another;

To whom have you shown honor this month? How?

Year One        20____

_____

_____

Year Two        20____

_____

_____

Year Three      20____

_____

_____

Year Four       20____

_____

_____

Year Five       20____

_____

_____

Notes

_____

_____

_____

**Ephesians 6:5-8** be obedient to those who are your masters…
in sincerity of heart, as to Christ; not with eyeservice, as men-
pleasers but as the servants of Christ, doing the will of God
from the heart;

Do you work diligently at all times or just when you are seen by others?

Year One        20____


Year Two        20____


Year Three      20____


Year Four       20____


Year Five       20____


Notes

# 25 MARCH

**1 Corinthians 10:31** Whether therefore you eat, or drink, or whatever you do, do all to the glory of God.

How/when have you glorified God at a meal?

**Year One**       20\_\_\_\_

**Year Two**       20\_\_\_\_

**Year Three**       20\_\_\_\_

**Year Four**       20\_\_\_\_

**Year Five**       20\_\_\_\_

**Notes**

**Luke 6:27** Love your enemies; do good to those who hate you.

What good have you done for someone who hates you?

Year One 20____

Year Two 20____

Year Three 20____

Year Four 20____

Year Five 20____

Notes

# 27 MARCH

**James 1:27** pure religion and undefiled before God and the Father is this, to visit the fatherless and widows in their affliction, and to keep him unspotted from the world

When was the last time you helped the less fortunate?

Year One          20____

_____

_____

Year Two          20____

_____

_____

Year Three        20____

_____

_____

Year Four         20____

_____

_____

Year Five         20____

_____

_____

_____

Notes

_____

_____

_____

**Ecclesiastes 12:14** For God shall bring every work into judgment, with every secret thing, whether it be good, or whether it be evil.

Do you have secret things that you don't even want to write in a private journal? Will you work on them? Starting when?

**Year One**      20____

_____

_____

**Year Two**      20____

_____

_____

**Year Three**    20____

_____

_____

**Year Four**     20____

_____

_____

**Year Five**     20____

_____

_____

**Notes**

_____

_____

# 29 MARCH

**Proverbs 17:17** A friend loves at all times, and a brother is born for adversity.

What person do you go to when you have problems? Do you have a friend that can count on you no matter what? Are you such a friend to someone?

Year One          20____

_____

_____

Year Two          20____

_____

_____

Year Three          20____

_____

_____

Year Four          20____

_____

_____

Year Five          20____

_____

_____

Notes

_____

_____

**1 Corinthians 13:13** And now remains faith, hope, love, these three; but the greatest of these is love.

We often talk of love, but what do you hope for right now, for hope is also great?

Year One        20____

Year Two        20____

Year Three      20____

Year Four       20____

Year Five       20____

Notes

**Deuteronomy 32:** 4 He is the Rock, his work is perfect: for all his ways are judgment: a God of truth and without iniquity, just and right is he.

How is God like a rock to you?

**Year One**        20____

_____

_____

**Year Two**        20____

_____

_____

**Year Three**      20____

_____

_____

**Year Four**       20____

_____

_____

**Year Five**       20____

_____

_____

**Notes**

_____

_____

_____

**Proverbs 10:23** It is as sport to a fool to do mischief: but a man of understanding hath wisdom.

Do you laugh at wrong doing or dirty jokes?

Year One 20____

Year Two 20____

Year Three 20____

Year Four 20____

Year Five 20____

Notes

# 2 APRIL

**Galatians 6:2** Bear you one another's burdens, and so fulfill the law of Christ.

When was the last time you eased another's problem or burden? What did you do?

**Year One**        20____

_____

_____

**Year Two**        20____

_____

_____

**Year Three**      20____

_____

_____

**Year Four**       20____

_____

_____

**Year Five**       20____

_____

_____

**Notes**

_____

_____

_____

**Romans 8:24** For we are saved by hope: but hope that is seen is not hope: for what a man sees, why does he yet hope for? But if we hope for that we see not, then do we with patience wait for it.

How has your hope saved you?

**Year One**      20____

**Year Two**      20____

**Year Three**   20____

**Year Four**    20____

**Year Five**     20____

**Notes**

# 4 APRIL

**2 Corinthians 5:17** Therefore if any man be in Christ, he is a new creature: old things are passed away; behold, all things are become new

How has your faith changed you?

Year One          20____

_____

_____

Year Two          20____

_____

_____

Year Three        20____

_____

_____

Year Four         20____

_____

_____

Year Five         20____

_____

_____

Notes

_____

_____

**Deuteronomy 31:8** And the LORD, he it is that does go before you; he will be with you, he will not fail you, neither forsake you: fear not, neither be dismayed.

Do you follow the Lord or do you try to go before him? In what way?

Year One          20____

Year Two          20____

Year Three       20____

Year Four         20____

Year Five         20____

Notes

# 6 APRIL

**Isaiah 43:1** But now thus said the LORD that created you, O Jacob, and he that formed you, O Israel, Fear not: for I have redeemed you, I have called you by your name; you are mine.

Do you feel the Lord is calling you to do anything? What is it?

Year One          20____

_____

_____

Year Two          20____

_____

_____

Year Three        20____

_____

_____

Year Four         20____

_____

_____

Year Five         20____

_____

_____

Notes

_____

_____

**Romans 5:5** The love of God is poured in our hearts by the Holy Spirit which is given to us.

Do you feel God's love within your heart? How did you last show it?

**Year One**     20____

**Year Two**     20____

**Year Three**     20____

**Year Four**     20____

**Year Five**     20____

**Notes**

# 8 APRIL

**Psalms 73:26** My flesh and my heart may fail, but God is the strength of my heart and my portion forever.

What most recently has broken your heart?

**Year One**        20____

**Year Two**        20____

**Year Three**      20____

**Year Four**       20____

**Year Five**       20____

**Notes**

**Matthew 11:28-30** Come to me, all who labor and are heavy laden, and I will give you rest.

What is your greatest burden? Have you asked for help?

**Year One**     20____

**Year Two**     20____

**Year Three**   20____

**Year Four**    20____

**Year Five**    20____

**Notes**

**Psalms 37:8** Cease from anger, and forsake wrath. Fret not yourself in any wise to do evil.

Have you allowed yourself to get angry this week? Why?

Year One        20____

_____

_____

Year Two        20____

_____

_____

Year Three     20____

_____

_____

Year Four       20____

_____

_____

Year Five        20____

_____

_____

Notes

_____

_____

_____

**Galatians 5:22-25** But the fruit of the Spirit is love, joy, peace, patience, gentleness, goodness, faith, meekness, temperance: against such there is no law.

What has given you a deep joy this week?

Year One        20____

Year Two        20____

Year Three      20____

Year Four       20____

Year Five       20____

Notes

# 12 APRIL

**Ephesians 4:26** Be angry, but sin not: let not the sun go down upon your wrath.

You may have been angry but did you forgive someone before the day was through?

Year One        20____

_____

_____

Year Two        20____

_____

_____

Year Three      20____

_____

_____

Year Four       20____

_____

_____

Year Five       20____

_____

_____

Notes

_____

_____

_____

**Philippians 4:6** Be anxious for nothing, but in everything by prayer and supplication with thanksgiving let your requests be made known to God

The last time you prayed, what did you give thanks for?

Year One       20____

Year Two       20____

Year Three     20____

Year Four      20____

Year Five      20____

Notes

# 14 APRIL

**John 12:32** And I, if I be lifted up from the earth, will draw all men unto me.

How do you lift up Christ for others to see?

Year One        20____

Year Two        20____

Year Three      20____

Year Four       20____

Year Five       20____

Notes

**Romans 13:7** Render therefore to all their dues: tribute to whom tribute is due; custom to whom custom; fear to whom fear; honor to whom honor.

Did you pay your taxes? Were you honest?

Year One          20____

Year Two          20____

Year Three       20____

Year Four         20____

Year Five          20____

Notes

# 16 APRIL

**Isaiah 26:3-4** Open you the gates, that the righteous nation which keeps the truth may enter in. You will keep him in perfect peace, whose mind is stayed on you: because he trusts in you.

What do you trust the Lord to do this month?

Year One          20____

Year Two          20____

Year Three        20____

Year Four         20____

Year Five         20____

Notes

**Genesis 1:20** And God said, Let the waters bring forth abundantly the moving creature that has life, and fowl that may fly above the earth in the open firmament of heaven.

What do you think of when you see a bird in flight?

Year One        20____

Year Two        20____

Year Three      20____

Year Four       20____

Year Five       20____

Notes

# 18 APRIL

**John 6:35** And Jesus said to them, I am the bread of life: he that comes to me shall never hunger; and he that believes on me shall never thirst.

What bread do you eat to sustain you?

**Year One**          20____

_____

_____

**Year Two**          20____

_____

_____

**Year Three**       20____

_____

_____

**Year Four**         20____

_____

_____

**Year Five**          20____

_____

_____

**Notes**

_____

_____

_____

**Psalms 95:6** O come, let us worship and bow down; let us kneel before the LORD, our Maker

When did you last worship God as your maker? How?

Year One        20____

Year Two        20____

Year Three      20____

Year Four       20____

Year Five       20____

Notes

# 20 APRIL

**James 4:8** Draw near to God and he will draw near to you…

What do you personally do to draw near to God?

Year One        20____

_____

_____

Year Two        20____

_____

_____

Year Three        20____

_____

_____

Year Four        20____

_____

_____

Year Five        20____

_____

_____

Notes

_____

_____

_____

**Acts 6:8** And Stephen, full of grace and power, did great wonders and signs among the people.

Do you just receive grace or are you filled with it and share it with others?

**Year One**　　20_____

**Year Two**　　20_____

**Year Three**　　20_____

**Year Four**　　20_____

**Year Five**　　20_____

**Notes**

# 22 APRIL

**Ecclesiastes 9:7** Go your way, eat your bread with joy, and drink your wine with a merry heart; for God now accepts your works.

What activity have you done that you know for sure that God would approve of?

**Year One**      20____

_____

_____

**Year Two**      20____

_____

_____

**Year Three**      20____

_____

_____

**Year Four**      20____

_____

_____

**Year Five**      20____

_____

_____

**Notes**

_____

_____

_____

**Psalms 96:11-13** Let the heavens rejoice, and let the earth be glad;... for he comes to judge the earth: he shall judge the world with righteousness, and the people with his truth.

Will you be glad on the Day of Judgment? Glad of what?

Year One        20___

Year Two        20___

Year Three      20___

Year Four       20___

Year Five       20___

Notes

# 24 APRIL

**Luke 15:7** I say to you, that likewise joy shall be in heaven over one sinner that repents, more than over ninety and nine just persons, which need no repentance.

Have you rejoiced on someone's repentance? When?

Year One        20____

_____

_____

Year Two        20____

_____

_____

Year Three      20____

_____

_____

Year Four       20____

_____

_____

Year Five       20____

_____

_____

Notes

_____

_____

**Philemon 1:7** For we have great joy and consolation in your love, because the hearts of the saints are refreshed by you, brother.

Is there someone that refreshes your heart? How?

Year One        20____

Year Two        20____

Year Three      20____

Year Four       20____

Year Five       20____

Notes

# 26 APRIL

**Proverbs 10:28** The hope of the righteous shall be gladness: but the expectation of the wicked shall perish.

Do you expect good or evil today? What good or evil?

Year One          20____

_____

_____

Year Two          20____

_____

_____

Year Three        20____

_____

_____

Year Four         20____

_____

_____

Year Five         20____

_____

_____

Notes

_____

_____

**Psalm 119:160** Your word is true from the beginning: and every one of your righteous judgments endures forever.

How do you view the words of God? Give an example.

Year One        20____

Year Two        20____

Year Three      20____

Year Four       20____

Year Five       20____

Notes

# 28 APRIL

**Proverbs 2:20** That you may walk in the way of good men, and keep the paths of the righteous

Where do you think the path you are on now will lead you?

Year One        20____

_____

_____

Year Two        20____

_____

_____

Year Three      20____

_____

_____

Year Four       20____

_____

_____

Year Five       20____

_____

_____

Notes

_____

_____

_____

**Job 27:2-4** All the while my breath is in me, and the spirit of God is in my nostrils; My lips shall not speak wickedness, nor my tongue utter deceit.

Are there times where you have questioned God or do you trust him even during the tough times?

Year One        20____

_____

_____

Year Two        20____

_____

_____

Year Three      20____

_____

_____

Year Four       20____

_____

_____

Year Five       20____

_____

_____

Notes

_____

_____

# 30 APRIL

**Titus 2:7-8** In all things showing yourself a pattern of good works: in doctrine showing soundness, gravity, sincerity, Sound speech, that cannot be condemned

Is there anyone that looks to you as their role model? Who/ how?

Year One        20____

_____

_____

Year Two        20____

_____

_____

Year Three      20____

_____

_____

Year Four       20____

_____

_____

Year Five       20____

_____

_____

Notes

_____

_____

**1 John 3:16** Hereby perceive we the love of God, because he laid down his life for us: and we ought to lay down our lives for the brothers

How have you helped a fellow believer last month?

**Year One**      20____

**Year Two**      20____

**Year Three**    20____

**Year Four**     20____

**Year Five**     20____

**Notes**

# 2 MAY

**1 Corinthians 10:13** …God is faithful, who will not suffer you to be tempted above that you are able; but will with the temptation also make a way to escape, that you may be able to bear it.

What was your last temptation and what was your way out?

Year One        20____

_____

_____

Year Two        20____

_____

_____

Year Three      20____

_____

_____

Year Four       20____

_____

_____

Year Five       20____

_____

_____

Notes

_____

_____

_____

**Psalms 100:4** Enter into his gates with thanksgiving, and into his courts with praise: be thankful unto him, and bless his name.

Do you start your prayers with thanksgiving and praise or just requests?

Year One        20____

Year Two        20____

Year Three      20____

Year Four       20____

Year Five       20____

Notes

# 4 MAY

**Romans 12:4-7** For as we have many members in one body, and all members have not the same purpose.

Do you recognize that everyone has their own unique abilities? Name an example.

Year One         20____

_____

_____

Year Two         20____

_____

_____

Year Three       20____

_____

_____

Year Four        20____

_____

_____

Year Five        20____

_____

_____

Notes

_____

_____

**Ephesians 4:31** Let all bitterness and wrath and anger and clamor and evil speaking, be put away from you, and all malice

Do you hold any bitterness to another? What/ why?

Year One      20____

Year Two      20____

Year Three      20____

Year Four      20____

Year Five      20____

Notes

# 6 MAY

**Psalms 32:8** I will instruct you and teach you in the way you should go; I will guide you with my eye.

Where do you think your life is taking you? Where do you think God would want you to go?

Year One        20____

_____

_____

Year Two        20____

_____

_____

Year Three      20____

_____

_____

Year Four       20____

_____

_____

Year Five       20____

_____

_____

Notes

_____

_____

**1 Peter 3:21** The like figure whereunto even baptism does now save us… by the resurrection of Jesus Christ

What were you personally saved from?

Year One        20____

_____

_____

Year Two        20____

_____

_____

Year Three      20____

_____

_____

Year Four       20____

_____

_____

Year Five       20____

_____

_____

Notes

_____

_____

_____

# 8 MAY

**Proverbs 1:8-9** My son, hear the instruction of your father, and forsake not the law of your mother: For they shall be an ornament of grace to your head, and chains about your neck.

What lesson do you remember that was taught you from one of your parents?

Year One          20____

_____

_____

Year Two          20____

_____

_____

Year Three        20____

_____

_____

Year Four         20____

_____

_____

Year Five         20____

_____

_____

Notes

_____

_____

_____

**2 Corinthians 1:3-4** Blessed be God, even the Father of our Lord Jesus Christ, the Father of mercies, and the God of all comfort, who comforts us in all our tribulation that we may be able to comfort those who are in any trouble, with the comfort which we ourselves are comforted by God.

How have you comforted someone else recently?

**Year One**       20____

**Year Two**       20____

**Year Three**     20____

**Year Four**      20____

**Year Five**      20____

**Notes**

# 10 MAY

**Psalms 37:3** Trust in the LORD, and do good; so shall you dwell in the land and be fed.

What was the last good you did?

Year One          20____

_____

_____

Year Two          20____

_____

_____

Year Three       20____

_____

_____

Year Four        20____

_____

_____

Year Five        20____

_____

_____

Notes

_____

_____

_____

**Romans 15:13** Now the God of hope fill you with all joy and peace in believing, that you may abound in hope, through the power of the Holy Ghost.

In what do you have hope so that the Spirit may abound in you?

Year One          20____

Year Two          20____

Year Three       20____

Year Four         20____

Year Five         20____

Notes

# 12  May

**Galatians 5:22-25** But the fruit of the Spirit is love, joy, peace, patience, gentleness, goodness, faith, meekness, temperance: against such there is no law.

How is meekness a strength and not a weakness?

**Year One**        20____

**Year Two**        20____

**Year Three**      20____

**Year Four**       20____

**Year Five**       20____

**Notes**

**Romans 12:2** And be not conformed to this world: but be transformed by the renewing of your mind, that you may prove what is that good, and acceptable, and perfect, will of God

How is the world trying to change you so you conform to it?

Year One        20____

Year Two        20____

Year Three      20____

Year Four       20____

Year Five       20____

Notes

# 14 MAY

**1 John 4:18** There is no fear in love, but perfect love casts out fear. Because fear has to do with punishment, and He that fears has not been perfected in love.

What was the last fear you laid to rest due to love? Do you ever feel jealous?

Year One        20____

_____

_____

Year Two        20____

_____

_____

Year Three      20____

_____

_____

Year Four       20____

_____

_____

Year Five       20____

_____

_____

Notes

_____

_____

_____

**Proverbs 10:5** He who gathers in summer is a wise son, but he who sleeps in harvest is a son who brings shame.

Have you slept when you should have been working and doing good? What good do you plan for tomorrow?

Year One          20____

Year Two          20____

Year Three       20____

Year Four         20____

Year Five          20____

Notes

# 16 MAY

**Psalms 25:5** Lead me in your truth and teach me, for you are the God of my salvation; on you I will wait all the day.

Do you think God wants you to learn something? What?

Year One          20___

_____

_____

Year Two          20___

_____

_____

Year Three        20___

_____

_____

Year Four         20___

_____

_____

Year Five         20___

_____

_____

Notes

_____

_____

_____

**1 Peter 3:7** Likewise, husbands, dwell with your wives with understanding and knowledge

When was the last time you made an effort to understand your spouse/ friend?

**Year One**     20____

**Year Two**     20____

**Year Three**   20____

**Year Four**    20____

**Year Five**    20____

**Notes**

**Psalms 52:8** But I am like a green olive tree in the house of God. I trust in the mercy of God forever and ever.

How have you trusted God this week?

Year One      20____

_____

_____

Year Two      20____

_____

_____

Year Three      20____

_____

_____

Year Four      20____

_____

_____

Year Five      20____

_____

_____

Notes

_____

_____

_____

**James 1:12** Blessed is the man that endures temptation: for when he is tried, he shall receive the crown of life, which the Lord has promised to them that love him.

What do you think the crown of life is?

Year One        20____

Year Two        20____

Year Three      20____

Year Four       20____

Year Five       20____

Notes

# 20 MAY

**Psalms 119:76** Let, I pray you, your merciful kindness be for my comfort, according to your word to your servant.

What words of God give you the greatest comfort?

**Year One** 20____

_____

_____

**Year Two** 20____

_____

_____

**Year Three** 20____

_____

_____

**Year Four** 20____

_____

_____

**Year Five** 20____

_____

_____

_____

**Notes**

_____

_____

_____

**2 Corinthians 5:17** Therefore if any man be in Christ, he is a new creature: old things are passed away; behold all things are become new.

Have you left your past behind you? What new have your replaced it with?

Year One        20____

Year Two        20____

Year Three      20____

Year Four       20____

Year Five       20____

Notes

**Hebrews 6:10** For God is not unrighteous to forget your work and labor of love, which you have showed toward his name, in that you have ministered to the saints, and do minister.

Who did you minister/serve this month?

Year One        20____

Year Two        20____

Year Three      20____

Year Four       20____

Year Five       20____

Notes

**Philippians 4:8** Finally, brethren, whatever things are true, whatever things are honest, whatever things are just, whatever things are pure, whatever things are lovely, whatever things are of good report; if there be any virtue, and if there be any praise, think on these things.

What lovely things have you thought about this month?

Year One          20____

Year Two          20____

Year Three        20____

Year Four         20____

Year Five          20____

Notes

# 24 MAY

**Ecclesiastes 2:24-25** There is nothing better for a man, than that he should eat and drink, and that he should make his soul enjoy good in his labor.

In what part of your work do you find enjoyment?

Year One        20____

_____

_____

Year Two        20____

_____

_____

Year Three      20____

_____

_____

Year Four       20____

_____

_____

Year Five       20____

_____

_____

Notes

_____

_____

_____

**Colossians 3:14** But above all these things put on love, which is the bond of perfection.

How has love brought harmony to your life?

**Year One**       20____

**Year Two**       20____

**Year Three**     20____

**Year Four**      20____

**Year Five**      20____

**Notes**

# 26 MAY

**Proverbs 18:7** A fool's mouth is his destruction and his lips are the snare of his soul.

Have you said things you regret? What did you do about it?

Year One        20____
_____
_____

Year Two        20____
_____
_____

Year Three      20____
_____
_____

Year Four       20____
_____
_____

Year Five       20____
_____
_____

Notes
_____
_____
_____

**Proverbs 14:16** A wise man fears, and departs from evil: but the fool rages, and is confident.

Have you feared evil and found a way to escape from it?

Year One          20____

Year Two          20____

Year Three        20____

Year Four         20____

Year Five         20____

Notes

# 28 MAY

**Isaiah 40:31** Those that wait on the LORD shall renew their strength; they shall mount up with wings as eagles; they shall run, and not be weary; and they shall walk, and not faint.

What are you willing to wait for? What strength do you need for what you are waiting for?

Year One        20____

_____

_____

Year Two        20____

_____

_____

Year Three      20____

_____

_____

Year Four       20____

_____

_____

Year Five       20____

_____

_____

Notes

_____

_____

**2 Corinthians 12:9** My grace is sufficient for you: for my strength is made perfect in weakness.

Give an example of how you trust grace more than your own strength?

Year One        20____

Year Two        20____

Year Three      20____

Year Four       20____

Year Five       20____

Notes

# 30 MAY

**Romans 5:2-5** …we rejoice in our sufferings, knowing that suffering produces endurance, and endurance produces experience, and experience produces hope…

How has your suffering produced hope and endurance?

Year One        20____

Year Two        20____

Year Three      20____

Year Four       20____

Year Five       20____

Notes

**Philippians 4:10-11** But I rejoiced in the Lord greatly that now at last your care for me has flourished again; though you surely did care, but you lacked opportunity

Have you doubted someone's concern but then found later that it was genuine? Explain.

Year One        20____

Year Two        20____

Year Three      20____

Year Four       20____

Year Five       20____

Notes

# 1 JUNE

**1 Corinthians 9:24-25** Know you not that they which run in a race run all, but one receives the prize? So run, that you may obtain. And every man that strives for the mastery is temperate in all things. Now they do it to obtain a corruptible crown; but we an incorruptible.

What kind of discipline have you applied to running your spiritual race?

**Year One**     20____

_____

_____

**Year Two**     20____

_____

_____

**Year Three**   20____

_____

_____

**Year Four**    20____

_____

_____

**Year Five**    20____

_____

_____

**Notes**

_____

_____

_____

**Psalm 66:19-20** But truly God has heard me; he has attended to the voice of my prayer. Blessed be God, which has not turned away my prayer, nor his mercy from me.

What was your last answered prayer?

Year One        20____

Year Two        20____

Year Three      20____

Year Four       20____

Year Five       20____

Notes

# 3  JUNE

**1 Peter 4:10** As every man has received the gift, even so minister the same one to another, as good stewards of the manifold grace of God.

What do you think is your greatest gift? How do you use it for good?

**Year One**     20____

_____

_____

**Year Two**     20____

_____

_____

**Year Three**     20____

_____

_____

**Year Four**     20____

_____

_____

**Year Five**     20____

_____

_____

**Notes**

_____

_____

**Jeremiah 29:13-14** And you shall seek me, and find me, when you shall search for me with all your heart. And I will be found of you, said the LORD…

Where do you try to find God?

Year One        20____

Year Two        20____

Year Three      20____

Year Four       20____

Year Five       20____

Notes

**Psalms 23:1-2** The LORD is my shepherd; I shall not want. He makes me lie down in green pastures. He leads me beside still waters.

What is your greatest "want"? Is it really needed? How can you let go of that desire?

Year One     20____

_____

_____

Year Two     20____

_____

_____

Year Three     20____

_____

_____

Year Four     20____

_____

_____

Year Five     20____

_____

_____

Notes

_____

_____

**1 Peter 2:24** He himself bore our sins in his own body on the tree, that we, being dead to sins, should live to righteousness: by whose stripes you were healed.

Name something specifically you have been healed from?

Year One        20____

Year Two        20____

Year Three      20____

Year Four       20____

Year Five       20____

Notes

# 7 JUNE

**Proverbs 15:17** Better is a dinner of herbs where love is, than a stalled ox and hatred therewith.

When was that last meal where you felt true love and contentment?

**Year One** 20____

_____

_____

**Year Two** 20____

_____

_____

**Year Three** 20____

_____

_____

**Year Four** 20____

_____

_____

**Year Five** 20____

_____

_____

**Notes**

_____

_____

_____

**Proverbs 23:13** Withhold not correction from the child:

How were you corrected as a child? How do you correct others?

Year One        20____
_____
_____

Year Two        20____
_____
_____

Year Three      20____
_____
_____

Year Four       20____
_____
_____

Year Five       20____
_____
_____

Notes
_____
_____
_____

# 9 JUNE

**Ecclesiastes 7:25** I applied my heart to know, and to search, and to seek out wisdom, and the reason of things…

What do you do to seek wisdom and understanding?

**Year One**       20____

**Year Two**       20____

**Year Three**     20____

**Year Four**      20____

**Year Five**      20____

**Notes**

**Proverbs 31:10** Who can find a virtuous woman? For her price is far above rubies.

Have you been an excellent spouse or friend? How can you be better?

Year One        20____

Year Two        20____

Year Three      20____

Year Four       20____

Year Five       20____

Notes

# 11 JUNE

**Revelation 21:4** And God shall wipe away all tears from their eyes; and there shall be no more death, neither sorrow, nor crying, neither shall there be any more pain: for the former things are passed away.

What do you hope for after your death?

Year One          20___

_____

_____

Year Two          20___

_____

_____

Year Three        20___

_____

_____

Year Four         20___

_____

_____

Year Five         20___

_____

_____

Notes

_____

_____

_____

**Isaiah 43:2** When you pass through the waters, I will be with you; and through the rivers, they shall not overwhelm you; when you walk through fire you shall not be burned, and neither shall the flame kindle on you.

What threatens to overwhelm you or burn you?

Year One          20____

Year Two          20____

Year Three       20____

Year Four         20____

Year Five          20____

Notes

# 13 JUNE

**Hebrews 11:1** Now faith is the substance of things hoped for, the evidence of things not seen.

If faith comes from hope what have you hoped for so your faith can grow?

Year One          20____

Year Two          20____

Year Three          20____

Year Four          20____

Year Five          20____

Notes

**Song of** Solomon 2:4 He brought me to the banqueting house and his banner over me was love.

What kind of "flag" or "banner" do you display to others?

Year One          20____

_____

_____

Year Two          20____

_____

_____

Year Three        20____

_____

_____

Year Four         20____

_____

_____

Year Five         20____

_____

_____

Notes

_____

_____

_____

# 15  JUNE

**James 1:19-20** Why, my beloved brothers, let every man be swift to hear, slow to speak, slow to wrath: For the wrath of man works not the righteousness of God.

Do you seek first to listen? What have you postponed saying so you could think it over?

**Year One**      20____

**Year Two**      20____

**Year Three**      20____

**Year Four**      20____

**Year Five**      20____

**Notes**

**Genesis 12:1** Now the LORD had said to Abram, Get you out of your country, and from your kindred, and from your father's house, to a land that I will show you:

How does God help you cope with change?

Year One        20____

_____

_____

Year Two        20____

_____

_____

Year Three      20____

_____

_____

Year Four       20____

_____

_____

Year Five       20____

_____

_____

Notes

_____

_____

_____

# 17 JUNE

**Romans 8:38-39** For I am persuaded, that neither death, nor life, nor angels… shall be able to separate us from the love of God, which is in Christ Jesus our Lord.

Has the loss of someone or something made you question God? Who or what?

**Year One** 20___

_____

_____

**Year Two** 20___

_____

_____

**Year Three** 20___

_____

_____

**Year Four** 20___

_____

_____

**Year Five** 20___

_____

_____

**Notes**

_____

_____

_____

**Psalms 85:8** I will listen to what God the Lord says: for he will speak peace to his people, and to his saints and let them not turn again to folly

What is God trying to say to you?

**Year One** 20____

**Year Two** 20____

**Year Three** 20____

**Year Four** 20____

**Year Five** 20____

**Notes**

# 19 JUNE

**Deuteronomy 30:19** I call heaven and earth to record this day against you, that I have set before you life and death, blessing and cursing: therefore choose life.

How precious is life to you?

Year One        20____

_____

_____

Year Two        20____

_____

_____

Year Three      20____

_____

_____

Year Four       20____

_____

_____

Year Five       20____

_____

_____

Notes

_____

_____

_____

**Psalms 59:16** But I will sing of your power; yes, I will sing aloud of your mercy in the morning: for you have been my defense and refuge in the day of my trouble.

When was the last time you sang or voiced thanksgiving in the morning for being rescued from trouble?

Year One        20____

Year Two        20____

Year Three      20____

Year Four       20____

Year Five       20____

Notes

# 21 JUNE

**Hebrews 12:28** we receiving a kingdom which cannot
be moved, let us have grace, by which we may serve God
acceptably with reverence and godly fear

How have you served God this month?

Year One        20____

Year Two        20____

Year Three      20____

Year Four       20____

Year Five       20____

Notes

**1 Samuel 15:22** And Samuel said, Has the LORD as great delight in burnt offerings and sacrifices, as in obeying the voice of the LORD? Behold, to obey is better than sacrifice, and to listen than the fat of rams.

Which do you the most: obey or ask for forgiveness?

Year One        20____

Year Two        20____

Year Three      20____

Year Four       20____

Year Five       20____

Notes

# 23 JUNE

**John 8:36** If the Son therefore shall make you free, you shall be free indeed.

Are you free from your addictions or still enslaved to them?

**Year One**     20____

_____

_____

**Year Two**     20____

_____

_____

**Year Three**     20____

_____

_____

**Year Four**     20____

_____

_____

**Year Five**     20____

_____

_____

_____

**Notes**

_____

_____

_____

**Psalm 103:8-10** The LORD is merciful and gracious, slow
to anger, and plenteous in mercy. He will not always chide:
neither will he keep his anger forever. He has not dealt with us
after our sins; nor rewarded us according to our iniquities.

Do you find it strange that the sinners are not punished here and now?

Year One        20____

_____

_____

Year Two        20____

_____

_____

Year Three      20____

_____

_____

Year Four       20____

_____

_____

Year Five       20____

_____

_____

Notes

_____

_____

_____

# 25 June

**Romans 14:8** For whether we live, we live to the Lord; and whether we die, we die to the Lord: whether we live therefore, or die, we are the Lord's.

What is different about the way you live that is a result of you being the Lord's?

Year One          20____

_____

_____

Year Two          20____

_____

_____

Year Three       20____

_____

_____

Year Four         20____

_____

_____

Year Five          20____

_____

_____

Notes

_____

_____

**Matthew 6:1** Take heed that you do not your alms before men, to be seen of them: otherwise you have no reward of your Father which is in heaven.

When did you last give something to another without being seen?

Year One        20____

Year Two        20____

Year Three      20____

Year Four       20____

Year Five       20____

Notes

# 27 JUNE

**2 Corinthians 13:11** Finally, brothers, farewell. Be perfect, be of good comfort, be of one mind, live in peace; and the God of love and peace shall be with you.

Do you feel at peace? How or why not?

Year One          20____

Year Two          20____

Year Three        20____

Year Four         20____

Year Five         20____

Notes

**Colossians 3:15** And let the peace of God rule in your hearts, to which you were called in one body; and be thankful.

What are you thankful for- right now- today? How do you show it?

Year One        20____

Year Two        20____

Year Three      20____

Year Four       20____

Year Five       20____

Notes

# 29 JUNE

**Romans 15:13** Now the God of hope fill you with all joy and peace in believing, that you may abound in hope, through the power of the Holy Spirit.

Do you practice joy and peace so the Spirit can fill you with hope?

Year One        20___

Year Two        20___

Year Three      20___

Year Four       20___

Year Five       20___

Notes

**2 Corinthians 4:16-18** For which cause we faint not; but though our outward man perish, yet the inward man is renewed day by day.

Can you feel your physical body aging but your inner self gaining strength? How?

Year One        20____

Year Two        20____

Year Three      20____

Year Four       20____

Year Five       20____

Notes

# 1 JULY

**2 Corinthian 7:13** Therefore we were comforted in your comfort

When did you feel comforted because of another's good fortune?

Year One        20____

_____

_____

Year Two        20____

_____

_____

Year Three      20____

_____

_____

Year Four       20____

_____

_____

Year Five       20____

_____

_____

Notes

_____

_____

**Ephesians 5:15** Live life with a sense of responsibility, not as those who do not know the meaning of life but as those who do. (Phillips)

What is the meaning of life for you?

Year One         20____

Year Two         20____

Year Three       20____

Year Four        20____

Year Five        20____

Notes

# 3 JULY

**Psalm 62:5** My soul, wait you only on God; for my expectation is from him. He only is my rock and my salvation: he is my defense; I shall not be moved.

What are you waiting for?

**Year One**       20____

_____

_____

**Year Two**       20____

_____

_____

**Year Three**       20____

_____

_____

**Year Four**       20____

_____

_____

**Year Five**       20____

_____

_____

**Notes**

_____

_____

**Galatians 5:1** Stand fast therefore in the liberty with which Christ has made us free, and be not entangled again with the yoke of bondage.

What seeks to entangle you?

**Year One**        20____

**Year Two**        20____

**Year Three**      20____

**Year Four**       20____

**Year Five**       20____

**Notes**

# 5   JULY

**Acts 17:11** These were more noble than those in Thessalonica, in that they received the word with all readiness of mind, and searched the scriptures daily, to see if what Paul said was true.

Do you accept what your preacher says or do you check to make sure it is true?

**Year One**       20____

_____

_____

**Year Two**       20____

_____

_____

**Year Three**    20____

_____

_____

**Year Four**      20____

_____

_____

**Year Five**       20____

_____

_____

_____

**Notes**

_____

_____

_____

**Revelation 2:10** Fear none of those things which you are about to suffer.

What do you think you may suffer in the future? How do you overcome fearing it?

Year One        20___

Year Two        20___

Year Three      20___

Year Four       20___

Year Five       20___

Notes

# 7 JULY

**Jeremiah 17:7** Blessed is the man that trusts in the LORD, and whose hope the LORD is.

When have you trusted the Lord though others said you were foolish?

Year One        20____

_____

_____

Year Two        20____

_____

_____

Year Three      20____

_____

_____

Year Four       20____

_____

_____

Year Five       20____

_____

_____

Notes

_____

_____

**Psalm 34:17** The righteous cry, and the Lord hears, and delivers them out of all their troubles.

When was the last time you cried out to the Lord for help? How did help appear?

Year One        20____

Year Two        20____

Year Three      20____

Year Four       20____

Year Five       20____

Notes

# 9 JULY

**Isaiah 55:6** Seek the LORD while he may be found; call upon him while he is near.

Where do you feel near to the Lord? Where do you seek him?

Year One          20____

Year Two          20____

Year Three        20____

Year Four         20____

Year Five         20____

Notes

**Revelation 4:11** You are worthy, O Lord, to receive glory and honor and power: for you have created all things, and for your pleasure they are and were created.

Name one of God's great creations.

Year One        20____

Year Two        20____

Year Three      20____

Year Four       20____

Year Five       20____

Notes

# 11 JULY

**Colossians 3:21** Fathers, provoke not your children to anger, lest they be discouraged.

Have you discouraged your children or were you discouraged as a child? How?

**Year One**        20____

_____

_____

**Year Two**        20____

_____

_____

**Year Three**      20____

_____

_____

**Year Four**       20____

_____

_____

**Year Five**       20____

_____

_____

**Notes**

_____

_____

**Mark 6:31** And he said to them, Come you yourselves apart into a desert place, and rest a while:

When did you last go away to be alone with God?

Year One        20____

_____

_____

Year Two        20____

_____

_____

Year Three        20____

_____

_____

Year Four        20____

_____

_____

Year Five        20____

_____

_____

Notes

_____

_____

# 13 JULY

**Isaiah 6:3** And one cried to another, and said, Holy, holy, holy, is the LORD of hosts: the whole earth is full of his glory.

Where do you see God's glory?

**Year One**      20____

_____

_____

**Year Two**      20____

_____

_____

**Year Three**      20____

_____

_____

**Year Four**      20____

_____

_____

**Year Five**      20____

_____

_____

**Notes**

_____

_____

**Psalms 40:3** And he has put a new song in my mouth, even praise to our God: many shall see it, and fear, and shall trust in the LORD.

When did you last sing a song of praise outside of a church meeting?

Year One        20____

Year Two        20____

Year Three      20____

Year Four       20____

Year Five       20____

Notes

# 15 JULY

**Ecclesiastes 3:20** All go to one place; all are of the dust, and all turn to dust again.

What good have you done that will outlive your body?

Year One          20____

_____

_____

Year Two          20____

_____

_____

Year Three        20____

_____

_____

Year Four         20____

_____

_____

Year Five         20____

_____

_____

Notes

_____

_____

_____

**John 14:17-18** the Spirit of truth… You know him, for he dwells with you and will be in you. I will not leave you comfortless; I will come to you…

How do you feel God comforts you?

Year One 20____

Year Two 20____

Year Three 20____

Year Four 20____

Year Five 20____

Notes

# 17 JULY

**John 16:22** And you now therefore have sorrow: but I will see you again, and your heart shall rejoice, and your joy no man takes from you.

In what does your heart rejoice today?

**Year One**        20____
................................................................................
................................................................................

**Year Two**        20____
................................................................................
................................................................................

**Year Three**      20____
................................................................................
................................................................................

**Year Four**       20____
................................................................................
................................................................................

**Year Five**       20____
................................................................................
................................................................................

**Notes**
................................................................................
................................................................................

**Lamentations 3:22-23** It is of the LORD's mercies that we are not consumed, because his compassions fail not. They are new every morning: great is thy faithfulness.

How did you feel this morning? How do you plan on using this new chance?

Year One        20____

_____

_____

Year Two        20____

_____

_____

Year Three      20____

_____

_____

Year Four       20____

_____

_____

Year Five       20____

_____

_____

Notes

_____

_____

_____

# 19 July

**Philippians 4:13** I can do all things through Christ who strengthens me.

What do you want to do this week?

Year One        20____

_____

_____

Year Two        20____

_____

_____

Year Three      20____

_____

_____

Year Four       20____

_____

_____

Year Five       20____

_____

_____

Notes

_____

_____

**Hebrews 6:19** The hope we have as an anchor of the soul, both sure and steadfast

What do you hope in that anchors your soul?

Year One        20____

Year Two        20____

Year Three      20____

Year Four       20____

Year Five       20____

Notes

# 21 JULY

**Matthew 5:23-24** Therefore if you bring your gift to the altar, and there remember that your brother has ought against you; Leave there your gift before the altar, and go your way; first be reconciled to your brother, and then come and offer your gift.

Is there someone you should go to and be reconciled?

**Year One**      20____

_____

_____

**Year Two**      20____

_____

_____

**Year Three**    20____

_____

_____

**Year Four**     20____

_____

_____

**Year Five**     20____

_____

_____

**Notes**

_____

_____

_____

**2 Peter 3:9** The Lord is not slack concerning his promise, as some men count slackness; but is longsuffering to us, not willing that any should perish, but that all should come to repentance.

Are you glad that the Lord is patient with you? Do you show the same patience to others?

Year One        20____

Year Two        20____

Year Three      20____

Year Four       20____

Year Five        20____

Notes

# 23 JULY

**John 8:12** Then Jesus spoke again to them, saying, I am the light of the world: he that follows me shall not walk in darkness, but shall have the light of life.

Have you ever stumbled in the darkness? Was it a spiritual or physical darkness?

Year One        20____
_____
_____

Year Two        20____
_____
_____

Year Three        20____
_____
_____

Year Four        20____
_____
_____

Year Five        20____
_____
_____

Notes
_____
_____

**Hebrews 6:11-12** And we desire each one of you should show the same diligence… so that you may not be slothful…

What good do you do with enthusiasm, diligence and no complaints?

Year One        20____

Year Two        20____

Year Three      20____

Year Four       20____

Year Five       20____

Notes

# 25 JULY

**Titus 2:7-8** In all things showing yourself a pattern of good works: in doctrine showing soundness, gravity, sincerity, Sound speech, that cannot be condemned...

Is your speech always above reproach? Does anyone have ever have doubts about your sincerity?

Year One        20____

_____

_____

Year Two        20____

_____

_____

Year Three      20____

_____

_____

Year Four       20____

_____

_____

Year Five       20____

_____

_____

Notes

_____

_____

_____

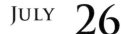
**Psalm 103:12** As far as the east is from the west, which is how far he removed our transgressions from us.

God can remove our transgressions but do you trust him enough to forgive yourself or still feel guilty?

Year One        20____

Year Two        20____

Year Three      20____

Year Four       20____

Year Five       20____

Notes

# 27 JULY

**Romans 10:1** Brethren, my heart's desire and prayer to God for Israel is that they might be saved.

Have you prayed for someone to be saved? Who, when?

Year One        20____

Year Two        20____

Year Three      20____

Year Four       20____

Year Five       20____

Notes

**Colossians 3:23-24** And whatever you do, do it with all your heart, as you would for the Lord and not men

Do you truly work as you are working for the Lord or just to be paid? Give a recent example.

Year One          20____

Year Two          20____

Year Three       20____

Year Four         20____

Year Five          20____

Notes

# 29 JULY

**Mark 16:16** He that believeth and is baptized shall be saved…

Have you been baptized? When? How did you feel?

Year One        20____

_____

_____

Year Two        20____

_____

_____

Year Three     20____

_____

_____

Year Four       20____

_____

_____

Year Five        20____

_____

_____

Notes

_____

_____

**1 John 3:18** My little children, let us not love in word, neither just in talk; but in deed and in truth

With what deed did you last show your love? To whom?

Year One          20____

Year Two          20____

Year Three        20____

Year Four         20____

Year Five         20____

Notes

# 31 JULY

**Philippians 4:6** Worry about nothing; but in everything by prayer and supplication with thanksgiving let your requests be made known to God

Have you learned to be more thankful in your prayers or just ask for more and more?

Year One        20____

Year Two        20____

Year Three      20____

Year Four       20____

Year Five       20____

Notes

**Romans 12:18** If it be possible, as much as lies in you, live peaceably with all men.

What have you done to make or maintain peace last month?

Year One        20____

Year Two        20____

Year Three      20____

Year Four       20____

Year Five       20____

Notes

# 2 AUGUST

**Romans 12:2** And be not conformed to this world: but be you transformed by the renewing of your mind, that you may prove what is that good, and acceptable, and perfect, will of God.

What can you do today or tomorrow that you are sure would please God?

**Year One**      20____

_____

_____

**Year Two**      20____

_____

_____

**Year Three**      20____

_____

_____

**Year Four**      20____

_____

_____

**Year Five**      20____

_____

_____

_____

**Notes**

_____

_____

_____

**Psalms 139:7-10** Where shall I go from your spirit? Or where shall I flee from your presence? If I ascend up into heaven, you are there: if I make my bed in hell, behold, you are there. If I take the wings of the morning, and dwell in the uttermost parts of the sea; even there shall your hand lead me, and your right hand shall hold me.

Do you feel the hand of God wherever you go, wherever you look? How?

Year One        20____

Year Two        20____

Year Three      20____

Year Four       20____

Year Five       20____

Notes

# 4 AUGUST

**Psalms 27:4-5** One thing have I desired of the LORD, that will I seek after; that I may dwell in the house of the LORD all the days of my life, to behold the beauty of the LORD, and to inquire in his temple.

What do you want to inquire of the Lord? What do you expect the answer will be?

**Year One**       20____

_____

_____

**Year Two**       20____

_____

_____

**Year Three**     20____

_____

_____

**Year Four**      20____

_____

_____

**Year Five**      20____

_____

_____

**Notes**

_____

_____

**Habakkuk 3:17-18** Although the fig tree will not blossom, neither will fruit be in the vines; the labor of the olive shall fail, and the fields will yield no meat; the flock will be cut off from the fold, and there will be no herd in the stalls: Yet I will still rejoice in the Lord, I will joy in the God of my salvation.

Do you still honor God when things go against you or do you grumble and complain?

**Year One**        20____

**Year Two**        20____

**Year Three**      20____

**Year Four**       20____

**Year Five**       20____

**Notes**

# 6 AUGUST

**Proverbs 10:9** He that walks uprightly walks surely: but he that perverts his ways shall be known.

Are your paths straight or crooked? What is the end of the path you have taken this week?

**Year One**       20____

_____

_____

**Year Two**       20____

_____

_____

**Year Three**       20____

_____

_____

**Year Four**       20____

_____

_____

**Year Five**       20____

_____

_____

**Notes**

_____

_____

**Luke 22:27** For who is greater, he that sits at meat, or he that serves? Is not he that sits at meat? But I am among you as one who serves.

Do you seek to serve or be served? How have you last served another?

Year One        20____

Year Two        20____

Year Three      20____

Year Four       20____

Year Five       20____

Notes

**Mark 9:50** Salt is good: but if the salt loses his saltiness, with which will you season it? Have salt in yourselves, and have peace one with another.

Is there a similarity between adding salt and making peace? What?

**Year One**        20____

---

**Year Two**        20____

---

**Year Three**      20____

---

**Year Four**       20____

---

**Year Five**       20____

---

**Notes**

---

**2 Corinthians 5:18-19** ...Christ, and has given us the ministry of reconciliation, To wit, that God was in Christ, reconciling the world to himself, not imputing their trespasses to them; and has committed to us the work of reconciliation.

Do you count offences or look for ways for reconciliation? How have you last tried to reconcile?

Year One        20____

Year Two        20____

Year Three      20____

Year Four       20____

Year Five       20____

Notes

# 10 AUGUST

**Romans 12:1** I beseech you therefore, brethren, by the mercies of God, that you present your bodies a living sacrifice, holy, acceptable unto God, which is your reasonable service.

Do you think your body is acceptable to God? Why/why not?

**Year One** 20____

**Year Two** 20____

**Year Three** 20____

**Year Four** 20____

**Year Five** 20____

**Notes**

**2 Timothy** 2:15 Study to show thyself approved unto God, a workman that does not need to be ashamed, rightly dividing the word of truth

When was the last time you really studied the word of God? Which verse or concept?

Year One        20____

Year Two        20____

Year Three      20____

Year Four       20____

Year Five       20____

Notes

**Romans 14:12-14** So then every one of us shall give account of himself to God. Let us not therefore judge one another anymore: but judge this rather, that no man put a stumbling block or an occasion to fall in his brother's way.

Have you recently judged another? Did you look to yourself first?

Year One        20____

_____

_____

Year Two        20____

_____

_____

Year Three      20____

_____

_____

Year Four       20____

_____

_____

Year Five       20____

_____

_____

Notes

_____

_____

**Matthew 8:24** And, behold, there arose a great tempest in the sea, so that the ship was covered with the waves: but he was asleep.

Do you have enough trust in God to sleep peaceably even in difficult times?

Year One        20\_\_\_\_

Year Two        20\_\_\_\_

Year Three      20\_\_\_\_

Year Four       20\_\_\_\_

Year Five       20\_\_\_\_

Notes

# 14 AUGUST

**Genesis 1:1** In the beginning God…

What major work have you started by first thinking about God?

Year One        20____

_____

_____

Year Two        20____

_____

_____

Year Three      20____

_____

_____

Year Four       20____

_____

_____

Year Five       20____

_____

_____

Notes

_____

_____

**Deuteronomy 31:8** And the LORD, he it is that does go before you; he will be with you, he will not fail you, neither forsake you: fear not, neither be dismayed.

Do you have any fear today? Why?

Year One      20____

Year Two      20____

Year Three      20____

Year Four      20____

Year Five      20____

Notes

**John 16:33** These things I have spoken to you, that in me you may have peace. In the world you have tribulation; but be of good cheer, I have overcome the world

What turmoil do you see in the world today?

Year One          20____

Year Two          20____

Year Three        20____

Year Four         20____

Year Five         20____

Notes

**2 Corinthians 1:3-4** Blessed be God and the Father of our Lord Jesus Christ, the Father of mercies, and the God of all comfort; Who comforts us in all our tribulation, that we may be able to comfort them which are in any trouble, by the comfort wherewith we ourselves are comforted of God

How have you been comforted? Have you tried to comfort another?

Year One        20____



Year Two        20____



Year Three      20____



Year Four       20____



Year Five        20____



Notes

# 18 AUGUST

**Proverbs 22:6** Train up a child in the way he should go: and when he is old, he will not depart from it.

What did your parent train you to do that you are still doing?

Year One        20____

Year Two        20____

Year Three      20____

Year Four       20____

Year Five       20____

Notes

**Psalms 23:4** Yea, though I walk through the valley of the shadow of death, I will fear no evil: for you are with me; your rod and your staff they comfort me.

What is the Lord's rod and staff to you? Hint: one corrects, one guides?

Year One          20____

Year Two          20____

Year Three        20____

Year Four         20____

Year Five         20____

Notes

# 20 AUGUST

**Proverbs 24:29** Say not, I will do so to him as he has done to me: I will render to the man according to his work.

Have you recently sought "pay back?" How did you respond?

Year One          20____

_____

_____

Year Two          20____

_____

_____

Year Three        20____

_____

_____

Year Four         20____

_____

_____

Year Five         20____

_____

_____

Notes

_____

_____

**Isaiah 41:13** For I the Lord your God will hold your right hand, and will say to you, Fear not; I will help you.

When was the last time you felt the hand of God help you?

Year One        20____

Year Two        20____

Year Three      20____

Year Four       20____

Year Five       20____

Notes

# 22 AUGUST

**Proverbs 31:20** She stretches out her hand to the poor; yes, she reaches forth her hands to the needy

What was the last thing you did to help the needy?

Year One          20____

_____

_____

Year Two          20____

_____

_____

Year Three        20____

_____

_____

Year Four         20____

_____

_____

Year Five         20____

_____

_____

Notes

_____

_____

**Ecclesiastes 3:1** To everything there is a season, and a time to every purpose under the heaven

Is there something you should do? What is the best time for doing it? When will you do it?

Year One        20____

Year Two        20____

Year Three      20____

Year Four       20____

Year Five       20____

Notes

# 24 AUGUST

**Jeremiah 29:11** For I know the thoughts that I think toward you, says the LORD, thoughts of peace, and not of evil, to give you an expected end.

Are you at peace within yourself right this moment? When have you been?

Year One        20____

Year Two        20____

Year Three      20____

Year Four       20____

Year Five       20____

Notes

**Psalms 63:2** To see your power and your glory, so as I have seen you in the sanctuary.

Where do you see God's power at work?

Year One        20____

_____

_____

Year Two        20____

_____

_____

Year Three      20____

_____

_____

Year Four       20____

_____

_____

Year Five       20____

_____

_____

Notes

_____

_____

# 26 AUGUST

**2 Corinthians 1:10** Who delivered us from so great a death, and does deliver: in whom we trust that he will yet deliver us;

From what do you hope the Lord will save you?

Year One     20____

Year Two     20____

Year Three     20____

Year Four     20____

Year Five     20____

Notes

**Psalms 33:20-22** Our soul waits for the LORD: he is our help and our shield. For our heart shall rejoice in him, because we have trusted in his holy name.

From what do you want the Lord to shield you? How do you think it will happen?

Year One        20____

Year Two        20____

Year Three      20____

Year Four       20____

Year Five       20____

Notes

# 28 AUGUST

**Proverbs 3:5-6** Trust in the LORD with all your heart, and don't lean on your own understanding. In all your ways acknowledge him, and he shall direct your paths.

How do you acknowledge the Lord? When did you last do it?

**Year One**      20____

_____

_____

**Year Two**      20____

_____

_____

**Year Three**    20____

_____

_____

**Year Four**     20____

_____

_____

**Year Five**     20____

_____

_____

**Notes**

_____

_____

**Philippians 3:14** I press toward the mark for the prize of the high calling of God in Christ Jesus.

What is your goal in life?

Year One        20____
_____
_____

Year Two        20____
_____
_____

Year Three      20____
_____
_____

Year Four       20____
_____
_____

Year Five       20____
_____
_____

Notes
_____
_____

# 30 August

**Psalms 7:11** God judges the righteous, and God is angry with the wicked every day.

Do you think you may have made God angry this month?

Year One        20____

Year Two        20____

Year Three      20____

Year Four       20____

Year Five       20____

Notes

**Mark 1:15** And saying, the time is fulfilled, and the kingdom of God is at hand: repent, and believe the gospel.

What is the gospel to you?

Year One          20____

Year Two          20____

Year Three        20____

Year Four         20____

Year Five         20____

Notes

# 1 SEPTEMBER

**John 6:27** Labor not for the meat which perishes, but for that meat which endures to everlasting life

Do you labor for food and shelter? How do you labor for things that endure the ages?

Year One          20____

_____

_____

Year Two          20____

_____

_____

Year Three        20____

_____

_____

Year Four         20____

_____

_____

Year Five         20____

_____

_____

Notes

_____

_____

**Ephesians 2:10** For we are his workmanship, created in Christ Jesus to good works, which God has before ordained that we should walk in them.

What is the last "good works" you did?

**Year One**     20____

**Year Two**     20____

**Year Three**   20____

**Year Four**    20____

**Year Five**    20____

**Notes**

# 3 September

**Psalms 118:24** This is the day which the LORD has made; we will rejoice and be glad in it.

What makes you glad today?

**Year One**     20____

_____

_____

**Year Two**     20____

_____

_____

**Year Three**     20____

_____

_____

**Year Four**     20____

_____

_____

**Year Five**     20____

_____

_____

**Notes**

_____

_____

**Romans 5:8** But God shows his love for us in that while we were still sinners, Christ died for us.

Do you feel loved by God?

Year One        20____

Year Two        20____

Year Three      20____

Year Four       20____

Year Five       20____

Notes

**Proverbs 17:17** A friend loves at all times, and a brother is born for adversity.

How has a friend helped you in adversity?

**Year One** 20____

_____

_____

**Year Two** 20____

_____

_____

**Year Three** 20____

_____

_____

**Year Four** 20____

_____

_____

**Year Five** 20____

_____

_____

**Notes**

_____

_____

_____

**2 Corinthians 7:10** For godly sorrow works repentance to salvation not to be repented of: but the sorrow of the world works death.

What are you sorry for? How has it changed you?

Year One        20____

Year Two        20____

Year Three      20____

Year Four       20____

Year Five       20____

Notes

# 7 SEPTEMBER

**Luke 22:61-62** And the Lord turned, and looked on Peter. And Peter remembered the word of the Lord, how he had said to him, Before the cock crows, you shall deny me thrice. And Peter went out, and wept bitterly.

Has there been a time you denied being a Christian or hid the fact? Do you plan on doing it again?

**Year One**        20____

**Year Two**        20____

**Year Three**      20____

**Year Four**       20____

**Year Five**       20____

**Notes**

**Genesis 18:14** …Is anything too hard for the Lord…

What is hard for you?

Year One          20____

_____

_____

Year Two          20____

_____

_____

Year Three       20____

_____

_____

Year Four         20____

_____

_____

Year Five          20____

_____

_____

_____

Notes

_____

_____

# 9 SEPTEMBER

**Proverbs 3:5** Trust in the LORD with all your heart; and lean not to your own understanding.

What have you started with simple trust and faith in the Lord?

Year One        20____

Year Two        20____

Year Three      20____

Year Four       20____

Year Five       20____

Notes

**John 14:26** But the Comforter, the Holy Spirit, whom the Father will send in my name, he shall teach you all things and bring to your remembrance all that I have said to you.

What spiritual thing do you remember from times past?

Year One        20____

Year Two        20____

Year Three      20____

Year Four       20____

Year Five       20____

Notes

**Psalms 37:4** Delight yourself also in the LORD: and he shall give you the desires of your heart.

What is your heart's desire?

**Year One**       20____

_____

_____

**Year Two**       20____

_____

_____

**Year Three**     20____

_____

_____

**Year Four**      20____

_____

_____

**Year Five**      20____

_____

_____

**Notes**

_____

_____

_____

**Philippians 1:6** Being confident of this very thing, that he which has begun a good work in you will perform it until the day of Jesus Christ:

What good work would you like to start or complete by year's end?

Year One          20____

Year Two          20____

Year Three        20____

Year Four         20____

Year Five          20____

Notes

# 13 September

**Psalms 22:1** My God, my God, why have you forsaken me? Why are you so far from saving me, from the words of my groaning?

Have you gone through dark times when you felt forsaken?

**Year One**       20____

**Year Two**       20____

**Year Three**     20____

**Year Four**      20____

**Year Five**      20____

**Notes**

**Psalms 25:9** The humble will he guide in judgment: and the humble will he teach his way.

Do you feel humble? Do you look for His way or go your own and then ask for help?

Year One          20____

Year Two          20____

Year Three        20____

Year Four         20____

Year Five         20____

Notes

# 15 SEPTEMBER

**Exodus 20:12** Honor your father and your mother, that your days may be long on the land that the LORD your God gives you.

How have you honored your parents?

**Year One**     20____

_____

_____

**Year Two**     20____

_____

_____

**Year Three**     20____

_____

_____

**Year Four**     20____

_____

_____

**Year Five**     20____

_____

_____

**Notes**

_____

_____

_____

**Philippians 2:3** Let nothing be done through strife or vainglory; but in lowliness of mind let each esteem others better than themselves.

Do you try to compare yourself to others? Who do you esteem better than yourself?

Year One        20____

Year Two        20____

Year Three      20____

Year Four       20____

Year Five       20____

Notes

# 17 SEPTEMBER

**Song of Solomon 1:2** Let him kiss me with the kisses of his mouth! For your love is better than wine.

When was your last kiss?

**Year One**        20____

_____

_____

**Year Two**        20____

_____

_____

**Year Three**      20____

_____

_____

**Year Four**       20____

_____

_____

**Year Five**       20____

_____

_____

**Notes**

_____

_____

_____

**Jeremiah 6:16** Thus said the LORD, Stand you in the ways, and see, and ask for the old paths, where is the good way, and walk therein, and you shall find rest for your souls. But they said, we will not walk therein

Do you look for any good in the old ways or do you go to the new/fashionable just because it is new?

Year One        20____

Year Two        20____

Year Three      20____

Year Four       20____

Year Five       20____

Notes

# 19 SEPTEMBER

**Psalms 139:7-12** Where shall I go from your Spirit? Or where shall I flee from your presence?

Have you tried to flee from or to God? How?

**Year One**         20____

**Year Two**         20____

**Year Three**       20____

**Year Four**        20____

**Year Five**        20____

**Notes**

**Isaiah 30:18** And therefore will the LORD wait, that he may be gracious to you, and therefore will he be exalted, that he may have mercy on you: for the LORD is a God of judgment: blessed are all they that wait for him.

Are you making the Lord wait for you or are you waiting for him?

Year One        20____

Year Two        20____

Year Three      20____

Year Four       20____

Year Five       20____

Notes

# 21 SEPTEMBER

**Deuteronomy 32:10** (of God and Jacob) He found him in a desert land, and in the waste howling wilderness; he led him about, he instructed him, he kept him as the apple of his eye.

When was the desert of your life or a time when you felt all alone?

**Year One**        20____

_____

**Year Two**        20____

_____

**Year Three**      20____

_____

**Year Four**       20____

_____

**Year Five**       20____

_____

**Notes**

_____

**Jeremiah 29:11** For I know the thoughts that I think toward you, said the LORD, thoughts of peace, and not of evil, to give you an expected end.

What do you think is the Lord's plan for you? What can you do to speed it along?

Year One        20____

Year Two        20____

Year Three      20____

Year Four       20____

Year Five       20____

Notes

# 23 S E P T E M B E R

**Matthew 18:12-14** How think you? if a man have an hundred sheep, and one of them be gone astray, does he not leave the ninety and nine, and goes into the mountains, and seeks that which is gone astray?

Who is in greatest need of your help? How can you help even if you have to leave your comfort zone?

**Year One**        20____

**Year Two**        20____

**Year Three**      20____

**Year Four**       20____

**Year Five**       20____

**Notes**

**Colossians 3:13** Forbearing one another, and forgiving one another, if any man have a quarrel against any: even as Christ forgave you, so also do you.

How have you forgiven another this month?

Year One        20____

Year Two        20____

Year Three      20____

Year Four       20____

Year Five       20____

Notes

# 25 SEPTEMBER

**Romans 8:31** What then shall we say to these things? If God is for us, who can be against us?

Who opposes your good works? Are they greater than He who is with you?

Year One        20____

_____

_____

Year Two        20____

_____

_____

Year Three      20____

_____

_____

Year Four       20____

_____

_____

Year Five       20____

_____

_____

Notes

_____

_____

**Deuteronomy 32:7** Remember the days of old, consider the years of many generations: ask thy father, and he will show you; ask your elders, and they will tell thee.

Have you asked your elders about the past and their viewpoints?

Year One          20____

Year Two          20____

Year Three        20____

Year Four         20____

Year Five         20____

Notes

**1 Thessalonians 5:13** …Be at peace among yourselves.

Do you feel at peace this very moment? Why/why not?

**Year One**        20____

**Year Two**        20____

**Year Three**      20____

**Year Four**       20____

**Year Five**       20____

**Notes**

**1 Corinthians 13:4-8** Love is patient and kind; love does not envy or boast;

When did you last lose your patience? Are you working to be better?

Year One        20____

Year Two        20____

Year Three      20____

Year Four       20____

Year Five       20____

Notes

# 29 SEPTEMBER

**Psalm 63:3** Because your loving kindness is better than life, my lips shall praise you.

What was the last praise you bestowed?

Year One          20____

_____

_____

Year Two          20____

_____

_____

Year Three        20____

_____

_____

Year Four         20____

_____

_____

Year Five         20____

_____

_____

Notes

_____

_____

_____

**Deuteronomy 6:6-7** And these words, which I command you this day, shall be in your heart: And you shall teach them diligently to your children, and shall talk of them when you sit in your house, and when you walk by the way, and when you lie down, and when you rise up.

What have you taught your child (or friend) about God? Do you have a plan to do so?

Year One        20____

Year Two        20____

Year Three      20____

Year Four       20____

Year Five       20____

Notes

# 1 OCTOBER

**Philippians 3:13-15** Brothers, I count not myself to have apprehended: but this one thing I do, forgetting those things which are behind, and reaching forth to those things which are before, I press toward the mark for the prize of the high calling of God in Christ Jesus.

Who helped you get where you are? Have you thanked them?

**Year One** 20____

**Year Two** 20____

**Year Three** 20____

**Year Four** 20____

**Year Five** 20____

**Notes**

**1 Timothy 6:17** Charge them that are rich in this world, that they be not haughty, nor trust in uncertain riches, but in the living God, who gives us richly all things to enjoy;

In what way are your rich?

Year One        20____

Year Two        20____

Year Three      20____

Year Four       20____

Year Five       20____

Notes

# 3 OCTOBER

**Psalms 46:1-3** God is our refuge and strength, a very present help in trouble. Therefore will not we fear, though the earth be removed, and though the mountains be carried into the middle of the sea…

How has God provided a refuge for you?

Year One          20____

Year Two          20____

Year Three       20____

Year Four         20____

Year Five          20____

Notes

**Romans 12:1** I beseech you therefore, brethren, by the mercies of God, that you present your bodies a living sacrifice, holy, acceptable unto God, which is your reasonable service.

How have you taken care of your body so you can best work for God?

Year One        20____

Year Two        20____

Year Three      20____

Year Four       20____

Year Five       20____

Notes

# 5 OCTOBER

**Psalm 95:2** Let us come before his presence with thanksgiving, and make a joyful noise to him with psalms.

What was the last thing you thanked God for?

Year One        20____

_____

_____

Year Two        20____

_____

_____

Year Three      20____

_____

_____

Year Four       20____

_____

_____

Year Five       20____

_____

_____

_____

Notes

_____

_____

_____

**1 Corinthians 14:15** What is it then? I will pray with the spirit, and I will pray with the understanding also: I will sing with the spirit, and I will sing with the understanding also.

What has your mind told you to pray for? Your spirit?

Year One        20____

Year Two        20____

Year Three      20____

Year Four       20____

Year Five       20____

Notes

# 7 OCTOBER

**Psalms 37:23-24** The steps of a good man are ordered by the LORD: and he delights in his way. Though he falls, he shall not be utterly cast down: for the LORD upholds him with his hand.

What have you tried and failed at but trusted God and tried again?

**Year One**　　　20____

**Year Two**　　　20____

**Year Three**　　　20____

**Year Four**　　　20____

**Year Five**　　　20____

**Notes**

**Luke 3:10-11** And the people asked him, saying, what shall we do then? He answers and said to them, He that has two coats, let him impart to him that has none; and he that has meat, let him do likewise.

What was your last donation to the poor? When was the last time you cleaned out your closet?

Year One        20____

Year Two        20____

Year Three      20____

Year Four       20____

Year Five       20____

Notes

# 9 OCTOBER

**1 Timothy 2:1-2** I exhort therefore, that, first of all, supplications, prayers, intercessions, and giving of thanks, be made for all men; for kings, and for all that are in authority; that we may lead a quiet and peaceable life in all godliness and honesty.

When was the last time you prayed for our leaders and for peace?

**Year One**     20\_\_\_\_

**Year Two**     20\_\_\_\_

**Year Three**     20\_\_\_\_

**Year Four**     20\_\_\_\_

**Year Five**     20\_\_\_\_

**Notes**

**Matthew 6:24-25** No man can serve two masters: for either he will hate the one, and love the other; or else he will hold to the one, and despise the other. You cannot serve God and mammon.

Have you let money dictate your actions when you knew better?

Year One        20____

_____

_____

Year Two        20____

_____

_____

Year Three      20____

_____

_____

Year Four       20____

_____

_____

Year Five       20____

_____

_____

Notes

_____

_____

_____

# 11 OCTOBER

**Ephesians 6:18** Praying always with all prayer and supplication in the Spirit…

When was the last time you prayed? What for?


**Year One** 20____

_____

_____


**Year Two** 20____

_____

_____


**Year Three** 20____

_____

_____


**Year Four** 20____

_____

_____


**Year Five** 20____

_____

_____


**Notes**

_____

_____

**Romans 12:2** And be not conformed to this world: but be you transformed by the renewing of your mind, that ye may prove what is that good, and acceptable, and perfect, will of God.

What do you do that is different from the way those of the world would do it?

Year One        20____

Year Two        20____

Year Three      20____

Year Four       20____

Year Five       20____

Notes

# 13 OCTOBER

**Leviticus 19:16** You shall not go up and down as a talebearer among your people: neither shall you stand against the blood of your neighbor; I am the LORD.

Have you gossiped or complained about another? Did you ask for forgiveness?

**Year One**        20____

_____

**Year Two**        20____

_____

**Year Three**      20____

_____

**Year Four**       20____

_____

**Year Five**       20____

_____

**Notes**

_____

**Mark 10:45** For even the Son of man came not to be ministered to, but to minister, and to give his life a ransom for many.

Have you served someone else who was "below you".

Year One        20____

Year Two        20____

Year Three      20____

Year Four       20____

Year Five       20____

Notes

# 15 OCTOBER

**Psalms 127:4-5** As arrows are in the hand of a mighty man; so are children of the youth. Happy is the man that has his quiver full of them: they shall not be ashamed, but they shall speak with the enemies in the gate.

If you have children, how have they enriched your life? If not, as a child, how have you come to the aid of your family?

**Year One**        20____

**Year Two**        20____

**Year Three**      20____

**Year Four**       20____

**Year Five**       20____

**Notes**

**Ephesians 2:10** For we are his workmanship, created in Christ Jesus for good works, which God has before ordained that we should walk in them.

What good works are you equipped to do? Are you doing it?

Year One        20____

Year Two        20____

Year Three      20____

Year Four       20____

Year Five       20____

Notes

# 17 OCTOBER

**Genesis 2:18** And the LORD God said, It is not good that the man should be alone;…

Do you ever feel alone? What do you do?

**Year One**       20____

_____

_____

**Year Two**       20____

_____

_____

**Year Three**     20____

_____

_____

**Year Four**      20____

_____

_____

**Year Five**      20____

_____

_____

**Notes**

_____

_____

_____

**Psalms 95:4-6** In his hand are the deep places of the earth: the strength of the hills is his also. The sea is his, and he made it: and his hands formed the dry land. O come, let us worship and bow down: let us kneel before the LORD our maker.

When did you last take time to just observe the majesty of nature?

Year One        20____

Year Two        20____

Year Three      20____

Year Four       20____

Year Five       20____

Notes

# 19 OCTOBER

**Psalms 30:5** …weeping may endure for a night, but joy comes in the morning.

In what did you first find joy in this morning?

**Year One**        20\_\_\_\_

.........................................................................................................................
.........................................................................................................................

**Year Two**        20\_\_\_\_

.........................................................................................................................
.........................................................................................................................

**Year Three**      20\_\_\_\_

.........................................................................................................................
.........................................................................................................................

**Year Four**       20\_\_\_\_

.........................................................................................................................
.........................................................................................................................

**Year Five**       20\_\_\_\_

.........................................................................................................................
.........................................................................................................................

**Notes**

.........................................................................................................................
.........................................................................................................................

**Psalms 18:33** He makes my feet like the feet of a deer, and sets me on my high places.

Do you feel secure and safe? What gives you that feeling?

Year One          20____

Year Two          20____

Year Three        20____

Year Four         20____

Year Five         20____

Notes

# 21 OCTOBER

**John 14:27** Peace I leave with you; my peace I give to you. Not as the world gives do I give to you. Let not your hearts be troubled, neither let them be afraid.

Is your heart right now, today, at peace and without fear? If not-what is the trouble?

**Year One**      20____

**Year Two**      20____

**Year Three**      20____

**Year Four**      20____

**Year Five**      20____

**Notes**

**1 Peter 4:19** Why let them that suffer according to the will of God commit the keeping of their souls to him in well doing, as to a faithful Creator.

What good have you done for others even while you yourself have suffered? Did it lift your spirit?

Year One          20____

Year Two          20____

Year Three          20____

Year Four          20____

Year Five          20____

Notes

# 23 OCTOBER

**Psalms 103:1-5** ...Bless the LORD, O my soul, and forget not all his benefits: Who forgives all your iniquities; who heals all your diseases; Who redeems your life from destruction; who crowns you with loving kindness and tender mercies; Who satisfies your mouth with good things; so that your youth is renewed like the eagle's.

Name a gift of kindness you have known?

**Year One**        20____

**Year Two**        20____

**Year Three**      20____

**Year Four**       20____

**Year Five**       20____

**Notes**

**Matthew 6:26** Behold the fowls of the air: for they sow not, neither do they reap, nor gather into barns; yet your heavenly Father feeds them. Are you not much better than they?

Have you gone hungry or in true need this year? Have you given thanks for what you have?

Year One          20____

Year Two          20____

Year Three        20____

Year Four         20____

Year Five         20____

Notes

# 25 OCTOBER

**Psalms 91:2** I will say of the LORD, He is my refuge and my fortress: my God; in him will I trust. I will say of the LORD

To you personally, what is the Lord's fortress?

Year One        20____

Year Two        20____

Year Three      20____

Year Four       20____

Year Five       20____

Notes

**John 9:1-3** ...He saw a man which was blind from his birth...
Jesus answered, Neither has this man sinned, nor his parents:
but that the works of God should be made manifest in him.

Give a time when you first judged but then your views of others changed
when you looked more closely.

Year One        20____

Year Two        20____

Year Three      20____

Year Four       20____

Year Five       20____

Notes

# 27 OCTOBER

**Romans 5:10** For if while we were enemies we were reconciled to God by the death of his Son, much more, now that we are reconciled, shall we be saved by his life.

God gave his son so we could be reconciled. What are you willing to give to be reconciled with another?

Year One        20____

_____

_____

Year Two        20____

_____

_____

Year Three      20____

_____

_____

Year Four       20____

_____

_____

Year Five       20____

_____

_____

Notes

_____

_____

_____

**Psalms 95:6** O come, let us worship and bow down: let us kneel before the LORD our maker.

When did you last humble yourself and worship God?

Year One        20____

Year Two        20____

Year Three      20____

Year Four       20____

Year Five       20____

Notes

# 29 OCTOBER

**Hebrews 4:16** Let us therefore come boldly to the throne of grace, that we may obtain mercy, and find grace to help in time of need.

When have you found grace in time of need?

**Year One**      20____

**Year Two**      20____

**Year Three**      20____

**Year Four**      20____

**Year Five**      20____

**Notes**

**Romans 2:6-7** Who will render to every man according to his deeds: To them who by patient continuance in well doing seek for glory and honor and immortality, eternal life:

Do you do your works with patience or do you sometimes lose patience with those you seek to help?

Year One        20____

Year Two        20____

Year Three      20____

Year Four       20____

Year Five       20____

Notes

# 31 October

**Psalm 43:3** O send out your light and your truth: let them lead me; let them bring me to your holy hill, and to your tabernacles.

Are you lead by the truth? How do you seek it?

**Year One**      20____

**Year Two**      20____

**Year Three**      20____

**Year Four**      20____

**Year Five**      20____

**Notes**

**Philippians 1:3** I thank my God in all my remembrance of you.

Who gives you joy when you remember them? Have you told them?

Year One        20____

Year Two        20____

Year Three      20____

Year Four       20____

Year Five       20____

Notes

# 2  NOVEMBER

**Proverbs 2:6** For the LORD gives wisdom; from his mouth come knowledge and understanding;

Where do you turn for wisdom and advice?

**Year One**  20____

_____

_____

**Year Two**  20____

_____

_____

**Year Three**  20____

_____

_____

**Year Four**  20____

_____

_____

**Year Five**  20____

_____

_____

**Notes**

_____

_____

**Matthew 6:14** For if you forgive others their trespasses, your heavenly Father will also forgive you. But if you forgive not men their trespasses, neither will your Father forgive your trespasses.

Do you hope that the Father will always forgive you? Do you always forgive others?

Year One       20____

Year Two       20____

Year Three     20____

Year Four      20____

Year Five      20____

Notes

**Galatians 5:13** For, brothers, you have been called to liberty; only use not liberty for an occasion to the flesh, but by love serve one another.

Do you feel free and not embarrassed to show your love?

**Year One**        20___

_____

_____

**Year Two**        20___

_____

_____

**Year Three**      20___

_____

_____

**Year Four**       20___

_____

_____

**Year Five**       20___

_____

_____

**Notes**

_____

_____

_____

**Mark 8:23-29** I see men as trees, walking ... he was restored, and saw every man clearly ... Jesus asked his disciples ... Whom do men say that I am? ... They answered....One of the prophets ... And he said to them, But whom do you say that I am? ... You are the Christ.

How is your spiritual eyesight? Do you see Christ as the Son of God or just a prophet?

**Year One**       20____

**Year Two**       20____

**Year Three**     20____

**Year Four**      20____

**Year Five**      20____

**Notes**

# 6 NOVEMBER

**James 5:13** Is any among you afflicted? Let him pray. Is any merry? Let him sing psalms.

What cheers you enough to make you sing?

**Year One**        20____

_____

_____

**Year Two**        20____

_____

_____

**Year Three**      20____

_____

_____

**Year Four**       20____

_____

_____

**Year Five**       20____

_____

_____

**Notes**

_____

_____

**2 Timothy 4:7** I have fought a good fight, I have finished my course, and I have kept the faith:

What "fight" have you finished for the Lord?

Year One        20____

Year Two        20____

Year Three      20____

Year Four       20____

Year Five       20____

Notes

# 8 NOVEMBER

**Exodus 17:12** But Moses hands were heavy; and they took a stone, and put it under him, and he sat thereon; and Aaron and Hur stayed up his hands, the one on the one side, and the other on the other side; and his hands were steady until the going down of the sun.

Have you helped someone who grew tired? Who? How?

**Year One**        20____

**Year Two**        20____

**Year Three**      20____

**Year Four**       20____

**Year Five**       20____

**Notes**

**John 15:13** Greater love has no one than this, that someone lay down his life for his friends.

Are you willing to die that others might live?

Year One        20____

Year Two        20____

Year Three      20____

Year Four       20____

Year Five       20____

Notes

# 10 NOVEMBER

**Acts 20:35** I have showed you all things, how that so laboring you ought to support the weak, and to remember the words of the Lord Jesus, how he said, It is more blessed to give than to receive.

What have you recently given? How did it make you feel?

Year One        20____

_____

_____

Year Two        20____

_____

_____

Year Three      20____

_____

_____

Year Four       20____

_____

_____

Year Five       20____

_____

_____

_____

Notes

_____

_____

_____

**Romans 14:1** Him that is weak in the faith receive you, but not to doubtful disputations.

Who have you welcomed at church? Did you set aside your differences?

**Year One**        20____

**Year Two**        20____

**Year Three**      20____

**Year Four**       20____

**Year Five**       20____

**Notes**

**Galatians 6:9** And let us not be weary in well doing: for in due season we shall reap, if we faint not.

Are there times you feel like giving up? When?

**Year One**       20____

**Year Two**       20____

**Year Three**     20____

**Year Four**      20____

**Year Five**      20____

**Notes**

**Psalms 28:7** The LORD is my strength and my shield; my heart trusted in him, and I am helped: therefore my heart greatly rejoices; and with my song will I praise him.

What has the Lord shielded you from?

Year One        20____

Year Two        20____

Year Three      20____

Year Four       20____

Year Five       20____

Notes

# 14 NOVEMBER

**Ephesians 2:10** For we are his workmanship, created in Christ Jesus for good works, which God prepared beforehand, that we should walk in them.

What good works do you think you are uniquely suited for?

Year One        20____

_____

_____

Year Two        20____

_____

_____

Year Three      20____

_____

_____

Year Four       20____

_____

_____

Year Five       20____

_____

_____

Notes

_____

_____

**2 Chronicles 7:14** if my people who are called by my name humble themselves, and pray and seek my face and turn from their wicked ways, then I will hear from heaven and will forgive their sin and heal their land.

When was the last time you humbled yourself and prayed?

Year One        20____

Year Two        20____

Year Three      20____

Year Four       20____

Year Five       20____

Notes

**Psalms 5:8** Lead me, O LORD, in your righteousness because of my enemies; make your way straight before me.

In what way do you hope the LORD will help straighten your path?

**Year One**　　20____

**Year Two**　　20____

**Year Three**　　20____

**Year Four**　　20____

**Year Five**　　20____

**Notes**

**Mark 1:7** (John the Baptist) And he preached, saying, There comes one mightier than I after me, the lace of whose shoes I am not worthy to stoop down and unloose.

Have you helped someone else do their job? Have you stepped aside for another?

Year One          20____

Year Two          20____

Year Three        20____

Year Four         20____

Year Five         20____

Notes

**Psalms 30:11-12** You have turned for me my mourning into dancing;

What do you feel like dancing about?

Year One         20____

_____

_____

Year Two         20____

_____

_____

Year Three       20____

_____

_____

Year Four        20____

_____

_____

Year Five        20____

_____

_____

Notes

_____

_____

_____

**Acts 17:26** And has made of one blood all nations of men for to dwell on all the face of the earth, and has determined the times before appointed, and the bounds of their habitation; That they should seek the Lord, if haply they might feel after him, and find him, though he be not far from every one of us:

How do you feel about people from other nations/races?

Year One        20____


Year Two        20____


Year Three      20____


Year Four       20____


Year Five       20____


Notes

**Romans 11:36** For from him and through him and to him are all things. To whom be glory forever. Amen.

Look around and notice the first thing that strikes your eye. Do you notice how it is from Him?

**Year One**      20____

_____

_____

**Year Two**      20____

_____

_____

**Year Three**      20____

_____

_____

**Year Four**      20____

_____

_____

**Year Five**      20____

_____

_____

**Notes**

_____

_____

**James 1:6** But let him ask in faith, nothing wavering. For he that wavers is like a wave of the sea driven with the wind and tossed.

Do you have doubts when you pray? About what?

Year One          20____

Year Two          20____

Year Three        20____

Year Four         20____

Year Five         20____

Notes

**Luke 17:15-19** And one of them, when he saw that he was healed, turned back, and with a loud voice glorified God, giving him thanks… And Jesus answering said, were there not ten cleansed? But where are the nine? There are not found that returned to give glory to God, save this stranger.

Have you thanked the Lord for his help? Is there someone in your past you have forgotten to thank?

**Year One** 20____

_____

_____

**Year Two** 20____

_____

_____

**Year Three** 20____

_____

_____

**Year Four** 20____

_____

_____

**Year Five** 20____

_____

_____

**Notes**

_____

_____

_____

**Philippians 2:4** Look not every man on his own things, but every man also on the things of others

What is the need of your closest friend and how can you help?

Year One         20____

_____

_____

Year Two         20____

_____

_____

Year Three       20____

_____

_____

Year Four        20____

_____

_____

Year Five        20____

_____

_____

Notes

_____

_____

_____

# 24 NOVEMBER

**Romans 12:12** Rejoice in hope, be patient in tribulation, continuing instant in prayer.

Are you constant in prayer?

**Year One**      20____

_____

_____

**Year Two**      20____

_____

_____

**Year Three**    20____

_____

_____

**Year Four**     20____

_____

_____

**Year Five**     20____

_____

_____

**Notes**

_____

_____

**Ephesians 6:5-7** …be obedient to those over your… Not with eye-service, as men pleasers; but as the servants of Christ, doing the will of God from the heart; With good will doing service, as to the Lord, and not to men:

Do you think you do your job well and done in a way that the Lord would approve?

Year One         20____

Year Two         20____

Year Three       20____

Year Four        20____

Year Five        20____

Notes

# 26 NOVEMBER

**Romans 8:28** And we know that all things work together for good to them that love God, to them who are the called according to his purpose.

What has worked out for the good that you first feared would not?

Year One          20____

_____

_____

Year Two          20____

_____

_____

Year Three        20____

_____

_____

Year Four         20____

_____

_____

Year Five         20____

_____

_____

Notes

_____

_____

**1 Peter 3:15** but sanctify the Lord God in your hearts: and be ready always to give an answer to every man that asks you the reason of the hope that is in you with meekness and fear.

What is the reason for your hope?

Year One        20___

Year Two        20___

Year Three      20___

Year Four       20___

Year Five       20___

Notes

# 28 November

**Psalms 3:3** But you, O LORD, are a shield about me, my glory, and the lifter of my head.

Why did you last have your head lowered? What caused you to lift it?

**Year One**        20____

_____

_____

**Year Two**        20____

_____

_____

**Year Three**      20____

_____

_____

**Year Four**       20____

_____

_____

**Year Five**       20____

_____

_____

**Notes**

_____

_____

_____

**Psalms 23:4** Yes, though I walk through the valley of the shadow of death, I will fear no evil: for you are with me; your rod and your staff they comfort me.

Do you trust the LORD even through death? Your death? The death of a love one?

Year One        20____

Year Two        20____

Year Three      20____

Year Four       20____

Year Five       20____

Notes

# 30 NOVEMBER

**Psalms 130:5** I wait for the LORD, my soul doth wait, and in his word do I hope.

What words of God give you greatest hope? What is your favorite verse?

Year One        20____

Year Two        20____

Year Three      20____

Year Four       20____

Year Five       20____

Notes

**James 1:12** Blessed is the man that endures temptation: for when he is tried, he shall receive the crown of life, which the Lord has promised to them that love him.

What trial or temptation have you gone through last month?

Year One        20____

Year Two        20____

Year Three      20____

Year Four       20____

Year Five       20____

Notes

# 2 DECEMBER

**John 4:23-24** But the hour comes, and now is, when the true worshippers shall worship the Father in spirit and in truth: for the Father seeks such to worship him. God is a Spirit: and they that worship him must worship him in spirit and in truth.

What does it mean to worship in truth?

**Year One**         20___

_____

_____

**Year Two**         20___

_____

_____

**Year Three**       20___

_____

_____

**Year Four**        20___

_____

_____

**Year Five**        20___

_____

_____

**Notes**

_____

_____

**Romans 12:2** And be not conformed to this world: but be you transformed by the renewing of your mind, that you may prove what is that good, and acceptable, and perfect, will of God.

How has God transformed your life?

Year One        20____

Year Two        20____

Year Three        20____

Year Four        20____

Year Five        20____

Notes

# 4 DECEMBER

**Ruth 1:16-17** And Ruth said, Entreat me not to leave you, or to return from following after you: for where you go, I will go; and where you lodge, I will lodge: your people shall be my people, and your God my God: Where you die, will I die, and there will I be buried: the LORD do so to me, and more also, if ought but death part you and me.

Do you follow and support your family? To you accept/tolerate your extended family?

**Year One**        20____

_____

_____

**Year Two**        20____

_____

_____

**Year Three**      20____

_____

_____

**Year Four**       20____

_____

_____

**Year Five**       20____

_____

_____

**Notes**

_____

_____

_____

**Micah 6:8** He has showed you, O man, what is good; and what does the LORD require of you, but to do justly, and to love mercy, and to walk humbly with your God?

What do you think God requires of you? How do you do it?

Year One          20____

_____

_____

Year Two          20____

_____

_____

Year Three        20____

_____

_____

Year Four         20____

_____

_____

Year Five         20____

_____

_____

Notes

_____

_____

_____

# 6 DECEMBER

**Joshua 1:9** Have I not commanded you? Be strong and of a good courage; be not afraid, neither be you dismayed: for the LORD your God is with you wherever you go.

When have you found yourself courageous for the Lord?

Year One          20____

_____

_____

Year Two          20____

_____

_____

Year Three        20____

_____

_____

Year Four         20____

_____

_____

Year Five         20____

_____

_____

Notes

_____

_____

**Jeremiah 26:14** As for me, behold, I am in your hand: do with me as seems good and meet to you.

How are you being molded in God's hands?

Year One        20\_\_\_

Year Two        20\_\_\_

Year Three      20\_\_\_

Year Four       20\_\_\_

Year Five       20\_\_\_

Notes

**Colossians 4:6** Let your speech be always with grace, seasoned with salt, that you may know how you ought to answer every man.

How do you season your speech? Give an example.

**Year One**        20____

_____

_____

**Year Two**        20____

_____

_____

**Year Three**      20____

_____

_____

**Year Four**       20____

_____

_____

**Year Five**       20____

_____

_____

**Notes**

_____

_____

_____

**Matthew 6:19-21** Lay not up for yourselves treasures on earth, where moth and rust does corrupt, and where thieves break through and steal: But lay up for yourselves treasures in heaven, where neither moth nor rust does corrupt, and where thieves do not break through nor steal: For where your treasure is, there will your heart be also.

What are your most precious treasures?

Year One        20\_\_\_\_

Year Two        20\_\_\_\_

Year Three      20\_\_\_\_

Year Four       20\_\_\_\_

Year Five       20\_\_\_\_

Notes

# 10 DECEMBER

**Psalm 94:19** In the multitude of my thoughts within me your comforts delight my soul.

What gives you the greatest consolation/comfort?

Year One        20____

_____

_____

Year Two        20____

_____

_____

Year Three      20____

_____

_____

Year Four       20____

_____

_____

Year Five       20____

_____

_____

Notes

_____

_____

**2 Corinthians 5:6-7** Therefore we are always confident, knowing that, whilst we are at home in the body, we are absent from the Lord: For we walk by faith, not by sight

Where/how have you walked by faith?

Year One        20____

Year Two        20____

Year Three      20____

Year Four       20____

Year Five       20____

Notes

# 12 DECEMBER

**Psalms 42:11** Why are you cast down, O my soul? And why are you disquieted within me? Your hope is in God: for I shall yet praise him, who is the health of my countenance, and my God.

Do you praise God even when your feel cast down and your sprit is disquieted?

**Year One**        20____

_____

_____

**Year Two**        20____

_____

_____

**Year Three**      20____

_____

_____

**Year Four**       20____

_____

_____

**Year Five**       20____

_____

_____

**Notes**

_____

_____

**1 Peter 5:5-6** …be clothed with humility: for God resists the proud, and gives grace to the humble. Humble yourselves therefore under the mighty hand of God, that he may exalt you in due time.

What was the last time you wanted to show your pride but were humble instead?

Year One         20____

Year Two         20____

Year Three       20____

Year Four        20____

Year Five        20____

Notes

# 14 DECEMBER

**Philippians 4:7** And the peace of God, which passes all understanding, shall keep your hearts and minds through Christ Jesus.

How has the peace of God guarded your heart?

**Year One**     20____

**Year Two**     20____

**Year Three**     20____

**Year Four**     20____

**Year Five**     20____

**Notes**

**Matthew 10:42** And whoever shall give to drink to one of these little ones a cup of cold water only in the name of a disciple, truly I say to you, he shall in no wise lose his reward.

What did you do the last time you did a simple act of kindness?

Year One        20____

Year Two        20____

Year Three      20____

Year Four       20____

Year Five       20____

Notes

# 16 December

**Hebrews 13:5** Let your conversation be without covetousness; and be content with such things as you have: for he has said, I will never leave you, nor forsake you.

Are you content with what you have? If not, why not?

**Year One**     20____

_____

_____

**Year Two**     20____

_____

_____

**Year Three**     20____

_____

_____

**Year Four**     20____

_____

_____

**Year Five**     20____

_____

_____

**Notes**

_____

_____

_____

**Psalms 143:10** Teach me to do your will; for you are my God: your spirit is good; lead me into the land of uprightness.

What do you think God's will is for you just today? Tomorrow?

Year One        20____
_____
_____

Year Two        20____
_____
_____

Year Three      20____
_____
_____

Year Four       20____
_____
_____

Year Five       20____
_____
_____

Notes
_____
_____

# 18 December

**Romans 1:20** For the invisible things of him from the creation of the world are clearly seen, being understood by the things that are made, even his eternal power and Godhead; so that they are without excuse:

Look around. What can you see from where you are sitting that shows God's eternal power?

**Year One**      20____

_____

_____

**Year Two**      20____

_____

_____

**Year Three**     20____

_____

_____

**Year Four**      20____

_____

_____

**Year Five**      20____

_____

_____

**Notes**

_____

_____

_____

**Romans 8:24-25** For we are saved by hope: but hope that is seen is not hope: for what a man sees, why does he yet hope for? But if we hope for that we see not, then do we with patience wait for it

For what do you patiently wait?

Year One        20_____

Year Two        20_____

Year Three      20_____

Year Four       20_____

Year Five       20_____

Notes

# 20 December

**Psalms 61:1-2** Hear my cry, O God; attend to my prayer. From the end of the earth will I cry to you, when my heart is overwhelmed: lead me to the rock that is higher than I.

When did you last feel your spirit being lifted up?

Year One         20____

Year Two         20____

Year Three       20____

Year Four        20____

Year Five        20____

Notes

**Psalm 34:18** The LORD is near to them that are of a broken heart; and saves such as be of a contrite spirit.

What was the last time your heart was broken?

Year One          20____

Year Two          20____

Year Three        20____

Year Four         20____

Year Five         20____

Notes

# 22 DECEMBER

**Matthew 5:44** But I say unto you, Love your enemies, bless them that curse you, do good to them that hate you, and pray for them which despitefully use you, and persecute you;

What good have you done for your enemies?

**Year One** 20____

_____

_____

**Year Two** 20____

_____

_____

**Year Three** 20____

_____

_____

**Year Four** 20____

_____

_____

**Year Five** 20____

_____

_____

**Notes**

_____

_____

_____

**Psalms 55:22** Cast your burden on the LORD, and he will sustain you; he will never permit the righteous to be moved.

What was the last burden you let the Lord carry for you?

Year One        20____

Year Two        20____

Year Three      20____

Year Four       20____

Year Five       20____

Notes

# 24 December

**Galatians 5:22-23** But the fruit of the Spirit is love, joy, peace, long-suffering, gentleness, goodness, faith, Meekness, temperance: against such there is no law.

When/how did you last show kindness to another?

Year One        20____

_____

Year Two        20____

_____

Year Three      20____

_____

Year Four       20____

_____

Year Five       20____

_____

Notes

_____

**Isaiah 9:6** For to us a child is born, to us a son is given; and the government shall be upon his shoulder, and his name shall be called Wonderful Counselor, Mighty God, Everlasting Father, Prince of Peace.

What have been the greatest gifts you have received this year? What is the greatest gift you have given?

Year One        20____

Year Two        20____

Year Three      20____

Year Four       20____

Year Five       20____

Notes

# 26 December

**Ephesians 3:20-21** Now to him that is able to do exceeding abundantly above all that we ask or think, according to the power that works in us, To him be glory in the church by Christ Jesus throughout all ages, world without end. Amen.

Has the Lord ever given you even more than you asked?

Year One        20____

_____

_____

Year Two        20____

_____

_____

Year Three      20____

_____

_____

Year Four       20____

_____

_____

Year Five       20____

_____

_____

Notes

_____

_____

**Psalms 19:1-3** The heavens declare the glory of God; and the firmament shows his handiwork. Day to day utters speech, and night to night shows knowledge. There is no speech nor language, where their voice is not heard.

What do you feel when you are alone on a starry night?

Year One        20____

Year Two        20____

Year Three      20____

Year Four       20____

Year Five       20____

Notes

**Luke 7:47-48** Why I say to you, Her sins, which are many, are forgiven; for she loved much: but to whom little is forgiven, the same loves little. And he said to her, your sins are forgiven.

Do you see others as sinners or as the forgiven with greater love?

**Year One**        20____

_____

_____

**Year Two**        20____

_____

_____

**Year Three**      20____

_____

_____

**Year Four**       20____

_____

_____

**Year Five**       20____

_____

_____

**Notes**

_____

_____

**Job 2:9** Then said his wife to him, Do you still retain your integrity? Curse God, and die.

Have there been dark times when you lost much and were ready to give up? What did you do?

Year One          20____

Year Two          20____

Year Three        20____

Year Four         20____

Year Five         20____

Notes

# 30 December

**2 Corinthians** 9:8 And God is able to make all grace abound toward you; that you, always having all sufficiency in all things, may abound to every good work.

What good work are you prepared to do next year?

Year One          20____

Year Two          20____

Year Three       20____

Year Four         20____

Year Five          20____

Notes

**Philippians 4:8** Finally, brothers, whatever things are true, whatever things are honest, whatever things are just, whatever things are pure, whatever things are lovely, whatever things are of good report; if there be any virtue, and if there be any praise, think on these things.

As you reflect on the year, have you tried to focus on the good things of the year?

Year One        20____

Year Two        20____

Year Three      20____

Year Four       20____

Year Five       20____

Notes

# REFLECTION - EVALUATION – RESOLUTION

**2 Corinthians 5:16-20** Why from now on know we no man after the flesh:… Therefore if any man be in Christ, he is a new creature: old things are passed away; behold, all things are become new. And all things are of God, who has reconciled us to himself by Jesus Christ, and has given to us the ministry of reconciliation;

That is: don't evaluate people by the world's standard of how they look or what they have. Realize that old things pass away. People change. You and I both need to realize that change happens. Forgive, reconcile your problems, hope, look at things through spiritual eyes, be thankful, trust God, and look for good things to do, look for the good in others… Be that new creature that God intended for you.

The question is: How do you hope to change?

**Year One** 20____

_____

_____

**Year Two** 20____

_____

_____

**Year Three** 20____

_____

_____

**Year Four** 20____

_____

_____

**Year Five** 20____

_____

# SPECIAL OCCASIONS
## YOUR BIRTHDAY

**Ecclesiastes 11:8** But if a man lives many years, and rejoices in them all;

How have you grown this year?

**Year One**       20____

_____

_____

**Year Two**       20____

_____

_____

**Year Three**     20____

_____

_____

**Year Four**      20____

_____

_____

**Year Five**      20____

_____

_____

# ANNIVERSARIES

**Ecclesiastes 4:9-12** Two are better than one; because they have a good reward for their labor. For if they fall, the one will lift up his fellow: but woe to him that is alone when he falls; for he has not another to help him up. Again, if two lie together, then they have heat: but how can one be warm alone? And if one prevail against him, two shall withstand him;

How have you helped and been helped by your mate this year?

Year One          20____

_____

_____

Year Two          20____

_____

_____

Year Three        20____

_____

_____

Year Four         20____

_____

_____

Year Five         20____

_____

_____

# BIRTHS

**1 Samuel 1:27-28** For this child I prayed; and the LORD has given me my petition which I asked of him: Therefore also I have dedicated him to the LORD; as long as he lives he shall be dedicated to the LORD

Are there plans/hopes for the child? Love, learning,...?

# WEDDINGS

**Ecclesiastes 4:9-12** Two are better than one; because they have a good reward for their labor. For if they fall, the one will lift up his fellow: but woe to him that is alone when he falls; for he has not another to help him up.

How do two help each other and become better together than apart?

# FUNERALS

**Psalm 34:18** The LORD is near to the brokenhearted;

How does you belief in God help you at times like these?

# GRADUATIONS

**Proverbs 19:21** There are many plans in a man's heart; nevertheless the counsel of the LORD, that shall stand.

What are your plans for the future? Do they include some service to God?

# Changes- Starting over

**Isaiah 43:18-19** Remember you not the former things, neither consider the things of old. Behold, I will do a new thing; now it shall spring forth; shall you not know it? I will even make a way in the wilderness, and rivers in the desert.

How do you plan on moving forward?

# A new home/dwelling

**Proverbs 24:3-4** Through wisdom a house is built; And by understanding it is established; And by knowledge the rooms are filled, with all precious and pleasant riches.

What is the most precious thing you want to fill your home with?

# Financial loss

**Hebrews 13:5-6** Let your life be without covetousness; and be content with such things as you have: for he has said, I will never leave you, nor forsake you. So that we may boldly say, The Lord is my helper, and I will not fear what man shall do to me.

What do you have that money cannot buy?

# Pain

**Proverbs 17:22** A merry heart does good like a medicine: but a broken spirit dries the bones.

What joy and hope can you focus on that makes you forget the pain?

# Author's parting comment

**3 John 1:2** Beloved, I wish above all things that you may prosper and be in health, even as your soul prospers.

27431235R00238

Made in the USA
San Bernardino, CA
12 December 2015